NATIONAL GEOGRAPHIC

Yosemite National Park Road Guide

THE **ESSENTIAL** GUIDE FOR MOTORISTS

by
Thomas Schmidt
maps by
Jeremy Schmidt

NATIONAL GEOGRAPHIC
WASHINGTON, D.C.

Founded in 1888, the National Geographic Society is one of the largest nonprofit scientific and educational organizations in the world. It reaches more than 285 million people worldwide each month through its official journal, NATIONAL GEOGRAPHIC, and its four other magazines; the National Geographic Channel; television documentaries; radio programs; films; books; videos and DVDs; maps; and interactive media. National Geographic has funded more than 8,000 scientific research projects and supports an education program combating geographic illiteracy.

For more information, please call 1-800-NGS LINE (647-5463) or write to the following address:

National Geographic Society
1145 17th Street N.W.
Washington, D.C. 20036-4688 U.S.A.

Log on to nationalgeographic.com; AOL Keyword: NatGeo.

Contents

Two women dance in the face of gravity high above Yosemite Valley, in this circa 1900 photo.

This book is dedicated to our children—Patrick, Colleen, and Kestrel—on whose behalf John Muir wrote the following prescient words a century ago:

"Everybody needs beauty as well as bread, places to play in and pray in, where Nature may heal and cheer and give strength to body and soul alike. This natural beauty-hunger is made manifest in the little window-sill gardens of the poor, though perhaps only a geranium slip in a broken cup, as well as in the carefully tended rose and lily gardens of the rich, the thousands of spacious city parks and botanical gardens, and in our magnificent National parks—the Yellowstone, Yosemite, Sequoia, etc.— Nature's sublime wonderlands, the admiration and joy of the world. Nevertheless, like anything else worth while, from the very beginning, however well guarded, they have always been subject to attack by despoiling gain-seekers and mischief-makers of every degree from Satan to Senators, eagerly trying to make everything immediately and selfishly commercial, with schemes disguised in smug-smiling philanthropy."

- John Muir, The Yosemite

How to Use This Guide

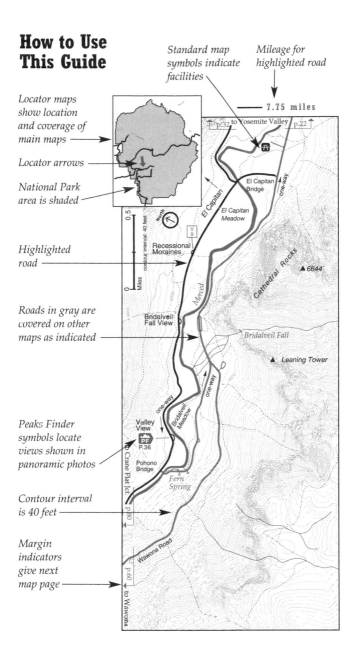

Locator maps show location and coverage of main maps

Locator arrows

National Park area is shaded

Standard map symbols indicate facilities

Mileage for highlighted road

Highlighted road

Roads in gray are covered on other maps as indicated

Peaks Finder symbols locate views shown in panoramic photos

Contour interval is 40 feet

Margin indicators give next map page

- Key map inside front cover gives page numbers for road maps.
- Map features and commentary run side by side.
- Maps generally run in sequence. Page numbers for adjoining maps are given in map margins— or refer to locator maps or key map.
- This book is a guide for motorists, not hikers or other backcountry users, who will find topographic maps and trail guides essential.

Land of Shining Rock

Acclaimed for its soaring granite cliffs, plunging waterfalls, and giant sequoia groves, Yosemite National Park encompasses a glorious swath of the Sierra Nevada range just 150 miles east of San Francisco. Established in 1890 and designated a World Heritage Site in 1984, the park's 1,200 square miles include thousands of lakes and ponds, two federally designated wild and scenic rivers, 800 miles of hiking trails, and 350 miles of roads. Although Yosemite is primarily a park renowned for its scenery, it is also a showcase of biological diversity, where elevations ranging from 2,000 feet to more than 13,000 feet bring five major life zones into relatively close proximity.

Made famous by such naturalists as John Muir and such photographers as Ansel Adams, Yosemite is one of the world's most frequently visited national parks. More than 3.5 million people flock here each year to admire its wildflower meadows, leaping waterfalls, colossal sequoia trees, and marquee landmarks including Half Dome, El Capitan, Bridalveil Fall, and Yosemite Falls. The bulk of visitation is concentrated within the seven square miles of the Yosemite Valley trough, which offers real challenges in terms of traffic on roads and trails. Fortunately, the park's efficient shuttle bus service and network of footpaths and bike trails makes it possible to avoid much of the congestion.

Compared with many mountain parks, Yosemite has a relatively simple geologic history. Virtually all of the rock one sees in the park is part of the Sierra Nevada Batholith, a vast body of magma that intruded, crystallized, and lay buried as granitic material beneath a very thick mass of overlying metamorphic rock. Geologists estimate that the batholith was positioned roughly six miles beneath the surface and that it took about 100 million years for its formation. Within the park, dozens of plutons of various ages and composition were emplaced. Some were intruded between 210 million and 150 million years ago, but most of the rock in Yosemite was thrust up between 120 million and 80 million years ago.

Opposite: This view of Yosemite Valley from Inspiration Point was published around 1859.

Subsequently, this entire region rose and has since been extensively eroded. Eventually, almost all of the overlying metamorphic rock was stripped away and the batholithic granites bared. The latest period of uplift occurred about 10 million years ago, causing the development of the Sierra Nevada range, with its distinct westward tilt, steep east face, and gentler western slopes.

As the gradient increased, so did the erosive power of westward flowing rivers and streams. The Merced gathered force and cut a narrow canyon in the rock 3,000 feet deep. By the onset of the Pleistocene ice age, the crest of the Sierra Nevada had reached an elevation of 14,000 feet.

At least four major periods of glaciation left their marks on the landscape of Yosemite. The most recent ended just 10,000 years ago; the earliest began perhaps a million years prior. Alpine glaciers formed along the crest of the range and coalesced into larger ice bodies as they moved down slope. Ice thickness in Yosemite Valley may have reached 4,000 feet during the early and most intense glaciation. The erosive power of moving ice studded with boulders and other debris widened existing valleys, steepened their walls, and deepened their floors. Virtually everywhere one looks in Yosemite today, one sees the effects of the glaciation.

Yosemite's dramatic elevation differences cause, within a relatively small area, a wide diversity of plant and animal communities. Of California's 7,000 plant species, about 20 percent can be found in Yosemite and 50 percent within the Sierra Nevadas. At the park's lowest elevations, roughly 2,000 to 4,000 feet, one finds the chaparral/oak woodland, a life zone characterized by plants such as the grey pine, blue oak, interior live oak, scrub oak, chamise, and toyon. Here live a host of small mammals such as the dusky-footed wood rat, birds such as the acorn woodpecker and the California thrasher, and most of the park's reptiles and amphibians. Mule deer browse here, bobcats hunt, and red-tailed hawks wheel overhead.

At the upper margin of this zone, the species blend with and then give way to the Lower Montane Life Zone, which one finds on the floor of Yosemite Valley. Here stands a mix of deciduous and evergreen trees: ponderosa pine, sugar pine, incense cedar, California black oak, canyon live oak, pacific dogwood, and cottonwood. This zone, which lies within the rough elevation boundaries of 4,000 feet to 7,000 feet, supports a wider range of mammals, including raccoons and ringtails, ground squirrels, mountain lions, mule deer, and black bear. The open meadows and surrounding forests provide good hunting for two owls of very different stature—the pygmy owl and the great-horned owl.

Around 6,000 feet, forest species of the Upper Montane Life Zone begin to take hold. These include the red fir, Jeffrey pine, western white pine, lodgepole pine, quaking aspen, and chinquapin. Flying squirrels live in these forests, along with long-tailed weasels, river otters, marmots, mule deer, and black bears.

Higher along the slopes of the Sierra, at roughly 8,000 feet, one reaches the Subalpine Life Zone, which receives more snow and where winter lasts longer than in any other zone in the park. Here, the lodgepole pine predominates, but forests are also characterized by whitebark pine and mountain hemlock. These trees form a band of thick forests along the lower reaches of the subalpine, but as one climbs still higher—say to about 10,000 feet—increasingly harsh climatic conditions crowd out even these hardy species, and usher in the challenging realm of the Alpine Life Zone.

Meadows in the Subalpine Zone—notably Tuolumne Meadows—support a vibrant, and ever-changing crush of wildflower species. Among the year-round residents are the water shrews, heather voles, Belding ground squirrels, and pikas; while larger mammals such as black bears, bighorn sheep, and mule deer (in summer) roam the area.

In addition to these broad life zones, Yosemite also harbors three scattered groves of giant sequoias—the Mariposa, Tuolumne, and Merced groves. Sequoias are the earth's largest and fastest-growing living things.

People have lived in the Yosemite region for thousands of years—perhaps 8,000 to 10,000 years. While the first people visited the area intermittently, about 4,000 years ago they began to settle. The most recent of these peoples are the Ahwahneechee, a branch of the Southern Sierra Miwok, who called the valley "Ahwahnee," meaning, "valley that looks like a gaping mouth." The Ahwahneechee traded roots, acorns, and manzanita berries with coastal tribes for abalone and other shells, and with the Mono Lake Paiute for obsidian, pine nuts, and rabbit-skin blankets.

Euro-American contact had little influence on the Ahwahneechee until the discovery of gold in 1848, when the mining ruined food sources and conflicts ensued. In 1851, the Mariposa Battalion followed Indian peoples into the valley and forced some into temporary exile. For the most part, though, the Ahwahneechee remained in Yosemite as the valley and the wider park became a tourist destination.

Early tourists came to Yosemite not only to see the "incomparable valley" but also the Mariposa Grove of giant sequoias. Inspired by the beauty of the place and worried about its possible exploitation, conservationists such as Frederick Law Olmsted and I. W. Raymond appealed to Congress for the protection of this land. On June 30, 1864, President Lincoln signed a bill entrusting Yosemite Valley and the Mariposa Grove to the state of California for public use and recreation. Later John Muir made a case to protect the High Sierra meadows from devastation wrought by livestock. His struggle resulted in federal legislation that created Yosemite National Park in 1890. Army units administered the wider park while California continued to govern the valley and the Mariposa Grove until 1906, when California ceded the grant lands back to the federal government.

Around the turn of the century, Hetch Hetchy Valley, which rivaled Yosemite Valley in terms of scenery, became the center of a bitter political battle. San Francisco wanted to dam the Tuolumne River as a source of drinking water. Muir and other opponents lost the battle in 1913, when Congress cleared the way for construction of O'Shaughnessy Dam.

Travelers' Information

Visitor centers, museums, and information stations, located throughout the park stock maps, brochures, and books. Some visitor centers offer interpretive films and exhibits. Park newspapers, available at entrance stations, list park services and seasonal schedules for ranger walks, talks, and other programs. Yosemite staff or volunteers are often on hand to answer questions, provide directions, and furnish updated information on road and campground conditions.

In the heart of hectic Yosemite Valley, the Valley Visitor Center stands just west of the main post office (shuttle bus stops #3 and #7) and has exhibits on the park's geology, common plants and animals, John Muir and the conservation movement, and the role of fire in the park's ecosystem. Nearby, the Yosemite Museum and Indian Village describe life among the Miwok and Paiute peoples and display historic paintings of park landscapes. The Ansel Adams Gallery exhibits not only that renowned photographer's work but also that of outstanding contemporary photographers and artists. More information, exhibits, and short nature walks are available at LeConte Memorial Lodge (shuttle bus stop #11) and the Nature Center at Happy Isles (shuttle bus stop #15).

The Tuolumne Meadows Visitor Center, open

seasonally, is located on the east side of the park along Tioga Road (Calif. 120). Information stations are located at Wawona, off Calif.

41 in the park's southwest corner, and at the Big Oak Flat Entrance, off Calif. 120 along the park's north-western border. Also at Wawona is the Pioneer Yosemite History Center, a cluster of historic buildings staffed by period reenactors.

Entrance fees for Yosemite are $20 per private vehicle, good for seven days. Individuals on foot, horseback, motorcycle, or bicycle pay $10 for a weekly permit. An annual pass for Yosemite costs $40. A National Parks Pass costs $50 and grants entry to all national parks for a year. A Golden Eagle Pass runs $65 and permits access to all national parks and monuments for a year. Golden Age Lifetime Passports for U. S. residents 62 or older cost $10, and Golden Access Passports for the disabled are free.

Correspondence and requests for information should be directed to: Superintendent, P.O. Box 577, Yosemite National Park, CA 95389-0577 (tel. 209-372-0200), *www.nps.gov/yose;* or Yosemite Association, Box 230, El Portal, CA 95318 (tel. 209-379-2648), *www.yosemite.org.*

Shuttle Bus Service: Free shuttle bus service is pro-vided and use encouraged throughout the eastern portion of Yosemite Valley year-round. In summer, free shuttle buses also run from Wawona to the Mari-posa Grove, and from Tioga Pass to Olmsted Point. Hikers' buses (fee) run daily to Glacier Point late spring through autumn and between Tuolumne Meadows and Yosemite Valley late June through Labor Day.

The shuttle bus system offers the only motorized access to the far eastern loop of the Yosemite Valley road system, and it offers the most practical motor-ized access to all points in the valley east of Camp 4 on Northside Drive, and east of Sentinel Bridge on Southside Drive.

Private vehicles loop through the valley all day and into the evening hours, but parking places are often difficult to come by after 10 a.m., especially at the valley's most popular sites. This can make touring by private vehicle frustrating. The hybrid-fuel buses, on the other hand, arrive frequently, stop within easy walking distance of all major sites, and are usually

Four sailors from The Ahwahnee, which during World War II was converted to a convalescent hospital, take in the sights at Tunnel View, circa 1944.

uncrowded. (Toward the end of the day, though, there may be standing room only as visitors wrap up their activities and head back to their own vehicles.)

Hiking: Driving is a good way to get an overall view of Yosemite, but a close-up look on foot is essential for a deeper understanding of the park and its environment. Besides, it's fun, and it's a good way to leave the crowds behind—at least on most trails. There are plenty of trails just off the roads. Some are short and have interpretive signs along the route or self-guiding booklets to help identify and explain interesting points.

Park naturalists lead a variety of hikes and strolls ranging in length from two to four hours. These excellent interpretive hikes are generally free and are conducted regularly throughout the park. See the park newspaper, *Yosemite Guide,* for a schedule.

No permits are required for day hiking, but some common-sense precautions are in order. Carry a trail map on all but the most popular short trails. Be prepared for sudden weather changes. Bring food and plenty of water. Do not drink from streams, lakes, or snowfields unless you treat or filter the water first. And please stay on the trails. Yosemite attracts so many visitors that even foot traffic can do lasting damage to the park's scenic treasures. For instance, soil compaction from foot traffic is one of the primary reasons oak trees have difficulty reproducing in Yosemite Valley, and high alpine meadows are supremely fragile.

Horseback Riding: Stables located in Yosemite Valley, Tuolumne Meadows, and Wawona offer trail rides spring through fall. They range from two hours to a full day, or even to an outfitted pack trip (tel. 209-372-8348).

Bicycling: Bicycling is permitted on paved roads throughout the park. More than 12 miles of paved bikeways wind though the eastern end of Yosemite Valley, offering visitors one of the most independent and carefree means of enjoying the park's most densely populated area. Another rewarding bike route follows the Old Big Oak Flat Road from the Tuolumne Grove to Hodgdon Meadow. (The old road is closed to motorized traffic.) Rental bikes are available at Yosemite Lodge and Curry Village. Bicyclists under age 18 must wear a helmet.

Fishing: A California sport fishing license is required for all persons 16 or older, and it must be attached to outer clothing and plainly visible. All lakes and reservoirs are open throughout the year. Special restrictions apply to some sections of rivers and streams.

Wheelchair Access: Visitor centers, art and nature centers, and some popular trails are accessible for people with wheelchairs. Visitors with disabilities can get an information packet and vehicle wheelchair-emblem placard (for special driving and parking privileges) at park entrances and information stations.

Seasons: Yosemite is open year round, but both the Tioga and Glacier Point roads close due to snow from about mid-November to late May. The summer season runs from June through September, with warm to hot weather, occasional rain, and lots of visitors. Rivers, and therefore waterfalls, reach their peak volumes in May or June. Wildflowers usually bloom abundantly during June in the park's lower elevations, but in Tuolumne Meadows the bloom often extends into midsummer.

Lodging: Reservations for all overnight lodging in Yosemite can be made by calling 559-252-4848, by writing to Yosemite Concession Services Corp., 5410 Home Ave., Fresno, CA 93727, or by booking online at *http://yosemitepark.com*. Rates in the park range from $67 per night for a tent-cabin at Tuolumne Meadows Lodge to $373 per night at The Ahwahnee. There are also High Sierra Camps; tent camps and cabins at

President Theodore Roosevelt, left, stands for a portrait with John Muir at Glacier Point in 1906.

Curry Village; and rooms and cabins at Yosemite Lodge. Caveat: Book early.

Camping: Yosemite has 13 campgrounds, with 7- to 14-day limits during summer. Fees range from $5 to $18 a night. Four campgrounds are open all year; the remainder are open from mid-spring to mid-fall or just for the summer. Demand is extremely high throughout the park for campsites of any kind. Visitors who want to camp in Yosemite during the height of the summer travel season should plan well in advance. They should either make reservations or arrive with the expectation that they may very well be turned away and have a backup plan.

Some of the campgrounds fill their sites on a first-come, first-served basis. They are: Bridalveil Fall, Camp 4/Sunnyside, Porcupine, Tamarack Flat, and Yosemite Creek. If one arrives early in the day, mid-week at these campgrounds, chances are fairly good that a site may become available. Chances thin considerably on the weekend.

Reservations are not required but are highly recommended at all other campgrounds during summer; contact the National Parks Reservation Service (tel. 800-365-2267 or online at *http://reservations.nps.gov).* Even without reservations, these campgrounds are worth checking, because people often forgo the reservations they have made or pull up stakes early, thus opening up vacancies. Most campgrounds fill those vacancies on a first-come, first-served basis and operate a waiting list that opens up first thing in the morning. Once the check-out deadline passes, unreserved vacant sites are assigned to those on the waiting list.

There are also several small national forest campgrounds near the eastern border of the park, but they also fill to capacity early in the day. Perhaps the national forest areas to the northwest of the park, Stanislaus or Humboldt-Toiyabe National Forests represent the best bet for those caught without a place to camp (*www. recreation.gov* or *www.reserveusa.com).* In those areas, dispersal camping is allowed: simply find a place to pull off the road and set up camp. Be sure the site you select is within national forest boundaries and not on private property.

Bears: Whether camping, hiking, climbing, or simply leaving your car behind for a while, take precautions to avoid problems with Yosemite's legendary black bears. Although the number of conflicts with bears has dropped dramatically in recent years, the park's ursine denizens still routinely break into vehicles, raid campsites, and swipe knapsacks and climbers' haul bags in a quest for human food. Campers are required to store food properly. In most cases that means that all food not in immediate use must be stored in the bear-proof lockers provided at every campsite. Similar lockers are provided at many of the park's trailheads where hikers and backpackers are required to empty their vehicles of food. Ice chests and other containers that look like they might contain food are to be kept out of sight in parked vehicles. Improper food storage is a violation subject to fines of up to $5,000.

Emergency: Dial 911.

Tourists enjoy the rustic 1920s comforts of Camp Curry.

On the Road

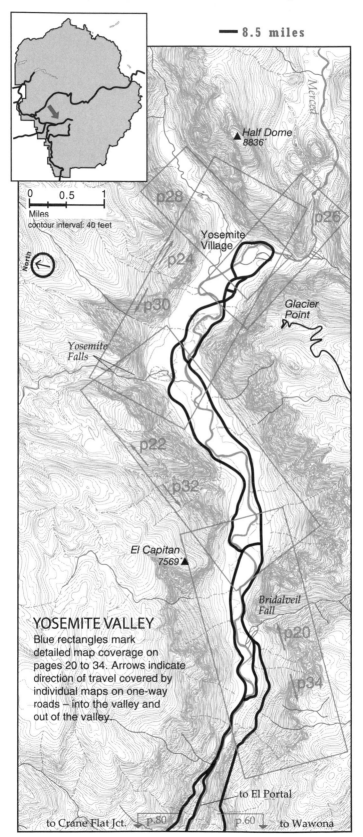

— 8.5 miles

0   0.5   1
Miles
contour interval: 40 feet

North

p28

p26

Yosemite Village

p24

Glacier Point

p30

Yosemite Falls

Half Dome
8836'

Merced

p22

p32

El Capitan
7569'

Bridalveil Fall

p20

YOSEMITE VALLEY
Blue rectangles mark detailed map coverage on pages 20 to 34. Arrows indicate direction of travel covered by individual maps on one-way roads – into the valley and out of the valley.

p34

to El Portal

to Crane Flat Jct.   p.80   p.60   to Wawona

18

Yosemite Valley

Valley Evolution: Perhaps the world's best-known example of a glacially carved canyon, Yosemite Valley frames some of the most celebrated landmarks in North America: Half Dome, El Capitan, Yosemite Falls, and continuous walls of neck-craning cliffs that rise 3,000 feet and more from the valley floor. While there is a timeless quality to this magnificent trench of granite, the valley as we know it is actually very young geologically—perhaps as young as 30,000 years.

Some 50 million years ago, the valley existed as a wide trough with the Merced River lazily meandering among rolling hills and hardwood forests. As the mountains of the Sierra were uplifted and tilted westward, the river accelerated and bit deeply into the landscape, eventually eroding a narrow, maze-like canyon that reached depths of 3,000 feet.

Then, beginning roughly a million years ago, a procession of Pleistocene glaciers engulfed the landscape, sometimes filling the valley to its brim, sometimes reaching only partway up its walls. The ice quarried the narrow, zig-zagging canyon into a straighter, broader, and deeper version of itself, with tributary streams stranded high above in hanging valleys. The bottom of the trough filled with glacial debris and sediments, which were shoved around by smaller and more recent glaciers. The last valley glacier melted just 10,000 years ago, leaving a moraine that dammed the Merced and created a shallow lake. The lake quickly filled in to form marshy bottomlands and meadows.

Merced River: Crystal clear and irresistible during the heat of summer, this splendid watercourse meanders the length of Yosemite Valley and offers a procession of heartbreaking swimming holes shaded by ponderosa pines, incense cedars, cottonwoods, and willows. The Merced starts high in the Clark Range along the southeastern margin of Yosemite Park, flows down Little Yosemite Valley, and stairsteps over Nevada and Vernal Falls before entering Yosemite Valley proper.

Yosemite Falls: The falls shifted to the present position about 130,000 years ago, when glacial activity in the hanging valley above deposited a moraine that diverted the flow of Yosemite Creek to the east. The old watercourse now forms a rather strenuous but well-traveled route to the Upper Fall (7.2-mile round trip; 2,700 vertical feet).

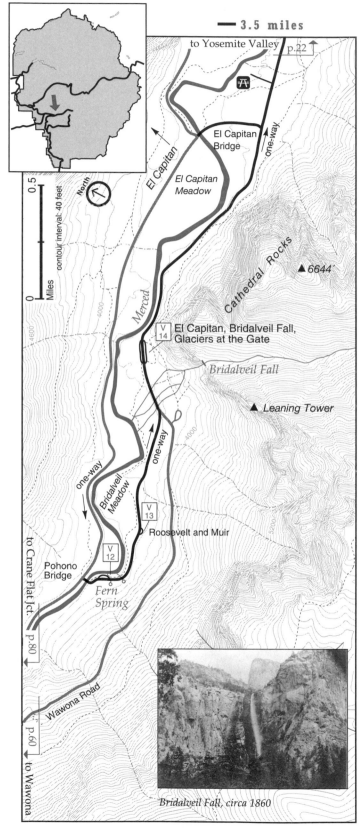

to Yosemite Valley p.22

El Capitan Bridge

El Capitan

El Capitan Meadow

one-way

North

contour interval: 40 feet

Merced

Cathedral Rocks

▲ 6644

V 14 El Capitan, Bridalveil Fall, Glaciers at the Gate

Bridalveil Fall

▲ Leaning Tower

one-way

one-way

Bridalveil Meadow

V 13

Roosevelt and Muir

V 12

Pohono Bridge

Fern Spring

to Crane Flat Jct.

p.80

Wawona Road

p.60

to Wawona

Bridalveil Fall, circa 1860

.5

0

Miles

4000

4600

4000

5200

Fern Spring: Shaded by tall incense cedars and big leaf maples, this small spring emerges from the forest floor as a glassy pool, splashes over mossy rock ledges, and crosses under the road. It resurfaces nearby amid a lush thicket of bracken ferns and then spills into a swift section of the Merced River. The spring's source consists of stream water that flows down the valley's high south walls, vanishes among talus fields, and percolates through forest soils to this point.

Roosevelt and Muir: Theodore Roosevelt and conservationist John Muir camped here in Bridalveil Meadow on May 17, 1903, as part of a three-day mule-packing trip Muir had arranged for the President. The pair discussed preservation issues, but mostly relaxed and enjoyed themselves. The President, an avid bird watcher, was surprised and a bit charmed to find that Muir took little interest in birds. He later wrote, "The hermit-thrushes meant nothing to him, the trees and the flowers and the cliffs everything."

El Capitan Viewpoint: As the road emerges from the forest, this massive brow of overbearing and particularly resistant granite swings into view and dominates the landscape. Exceedingly steep and largely unbroken, its face rises some 3,000 vertical feet from the valley floor. First climbed in 1958, the cliff is now stitched by more than a hundred routes. In early summer look to the left of El Capitan for Ribbon Fall, which drops 1,612 feet and is rated as the tallest free-leaping waterfall in Yosemite.

Bridalveil Fall: Bursting from the lip of a classic hanging valley, Bridalveil Fall plunges 620 vertical feet as a plume of vigorous white water and mist that, in Muir's words, "sways and sings in the wind." The right-hand slope of its granite cradle curves upward to a massive, overhanging prong of rock called Leaning Tower. A trail heads south through the oaks to the base of the fall and makes for a pleasant 0.8-mile round-trip stroll.

Glaciers at the Gate: An interpretive sign identifies a portion of a recessional moraine left by the last glacier to reside in Yosemite Valley. The moraine extends across the valley between the base of Cathedral Rocks and El Capitan, and it once acted as a dam that formed a shallow lake on the valley floor from this point east.

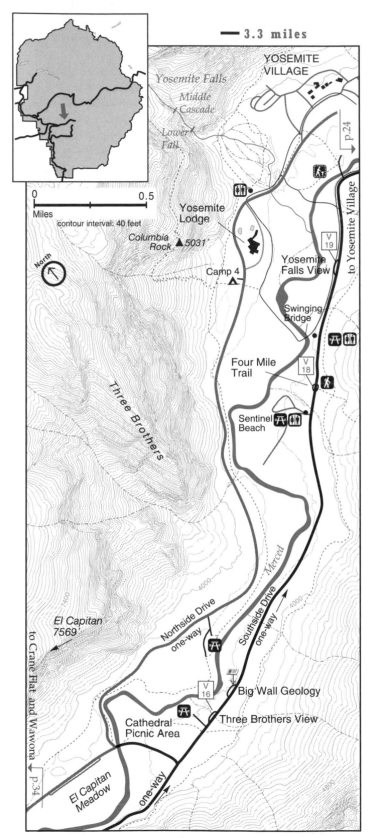

YOSEMITE VILLAGE

Yosemite Falls
Middle Cascade
Lower Fall

Yosemite Lodge

Columbia Rock ▲ 5031'

Camp 4

Yosemite Falls View

Swinging Bridge

Four Mile Trail

Sentinel Beach

Three Brothers

El Capitan 7569

Northside Drive one-way

Southside Drive one-way

Merced

Big Wall Geology

Three Brothers View

Cathedral Picnic Area

El Capitan Meadow

one-way

to Yosemite Village

→ p.24

V 19

V 18

V 16

to Crane Flat and Wawona ←

p.34 ←

North

0   0.5
Miles
contour interval: 40 feet

Cathedral Picnic Area: A short side road leads through incense cedars and ponderosa pines to a wide sand beach along the Merced River, which is shallow and gentle enough here for children to wade and swim. The site offers an extraordinary vista of El Capitan's south flank, which includes a dark, irregular splotch of intruded diorite nicknamed the "Map of North America." Turn around for a view of Cathedral Rocks and the twin pinnacles of Cathedral Spires, which stand about 2,000 feet above the valley floor.

Three Brothers Turnout: Just beyond the road to the picnic area, this turnout offers an excellent, cross-valley view of the Three Brothers, a series of three peaks, stacked and with parallel, west-facing slopes. They were named for the three sons of Tenaya, chief of the Yosemite tribe. The parallel faces reflect the effects of weathering along matching sets of joints.

Big Wall Geology: Here the sheer, squared-off profile of El Capitan protrudes high above the forest and catches early morning light. An interpretive sign discusses how the varying resistance of different types of granite help to determine valley scenery.

Sentinel Beach: Another pleasant swimming hole shaded by incense cedars, ponderosa pines, and cottonwoods, Sentinel Beach faces the backside of the Three Brothers and offers good views across the valley of Yosemite Falls and North Dome. Behind the beach and over the trees, Sentinel Rock towers 3,073 feet above the valley floor. The site is the landing point for all of the brightly colored Curry Village rafts that bob down the Merced in summer.

Four Mile Trailhead: A misnomer today, this trail climbs 3,220 feet in 4.8 miles to Union Point and Glacier Point. If that seems a bit strenuous, consider that early Yosemite visitors paid $1 each to hike the original (steeper) 4.0-mile trail. The route was surveyed in the 1870s by John Conway, a man who thought nothing of walking from the valley to Mariposa in a day. From the trailhead, there are good views of Sentinel Rock and, to its right, Sentinel Falls, a 2,000-foot springtime cascade.

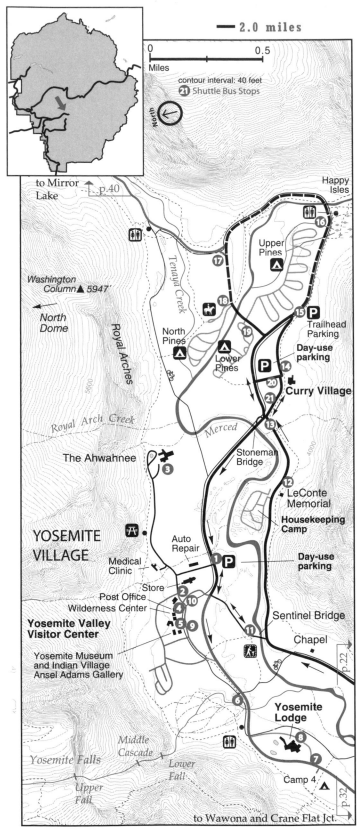

── **2.0 miles**

0   0.5
Miles

contour interval: 40 feet
㉑ Shuttle Bus Stops

North

to Mirror Lake   p.40

Happy Isles

Upper Pines

㉗   ㉖

Tenaya Creek

Washington Column ▲ 5947'

← *North Dome*

Royal Arches

North Pines

㉘

Lower Pines

㉙

㉕ P
Trailhead Parking

Day-use parking

P ㉔

㉚
㉑
Curry Village

5600

Royal Arch Creek

Merced

㉓

The Ahwahnee

㉓

Stoneman Bridge

4000

㉒
LeConte Memorial

Housekeeping Camp

YOSEMITE VILLAGE

🏕

Auto Repair

① P

Day-use parking

Medical Clinic

Store

Post Office
Wilderness Center

Yosemite Valley Visitor Center

Yosemite Museum and Indian Village
Ansel Adams Gallery

② ⑩
④
⑤ ⑨

⑪

Sentinel Bridge

Chapel

p.22

🚶

⑥

Yosemite Lodge

⑧

⑦

Middle Cascade

Yosemite Falls

Lower Fall

Camp 4 ▲

p.32

Upper Fall

to Wawona and Crane Flat Jct.

Yosemite Chapel: Built in 1879 and still in use, this steep-roofed interdenominational chapel originally stood near the Four Mile Trailhead. Sentinel Rock towers above its steeple. Mule deer and sometimes black bears feed in the meadow across the road. The Ahwahneechee periodically burned such meadows to prevent the spread of trees and to promote the growth of useful plants, such as grasses used for basketry. Much of Old Yosemite Village once stood in the meadow. Even after its buildings were removed, the settlement's buried trash discouraged natural plant growth. In 1993, the park service excavated the trash, and seeds that had lain dormant for more than 100 years have reclaimed the meadow.

Sentinel Bridge: This lovely granite bridge offers a classic view of Half Dome looming about 5,000 feet over an emerald-green bend of the Merced River. During the height of the Pleistocene ice ages, glaciers crested within 900 feet of Half Dome's summit and buried Yosemite Valley beneath more than 3,000 feet of moving ice.

LeConte Memorial: A Sierra Club shrine built in 1903 to commemorate geologist and explorer Joseph LeConte, this snug, stone block building served as Yosemite's first public visitor center. It still contains exhibits and a library and offers a variety of evening programs during summer. It stands directly across from Housekeeping Camp, a village of large canvas-wall tents that can be rented by park visitors.

Curry Village: Founded in 1899 as "Camp Curry" by David and Jenny Curry, the village provides lodging, meals, and rental bikes and rafts. The facilities lie directly below Glacier Point and, until 1968, acted as a nightly gathering spot to watch "Firefall," a tradition unique to Yosemite in which embers from a large fire set atop Glacier Point were shoved over the cliff.

Trailhead Parking: The sheer, north-facing cliffs of Glacier Point sweep upward from this point for more than 3,000 feet. Private cars (unless they have a handicap emblem) must either park here or double back. (To proceed east to Happy Isles or Mirror Lake, catch one of the frequent park shuttle buses.) Bears raid vehicles here, so take extra care with food storage.

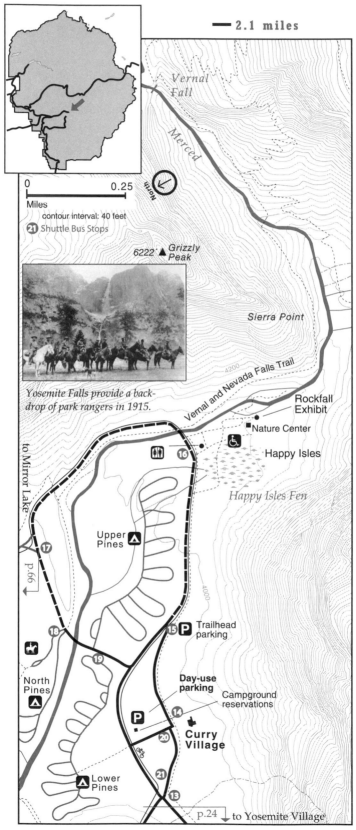

—— 2.1 miles

Vernal Fall

Merced

0 ——————— 0.25
Miles
contour interval: 40 feet
㉑ Shuttle Bus Stops

6222 ▲ *Grizzly Peak*

Sierra Point

Yosemite Falls provide a back-drop of park rangers in 1915.

Vernal and Nevada Falls Trail

Rockfall Exhibit

Nature Center

Happy Isles

Happy Isles Fen

to Mirror Lake

Upper Pines

⑰

← p.66

⑱

North Pines

⑲

⑮ P Trailhead parking

Day-use parking

Campground reservations

⑭

P

Curry Village

⑳

Lower Pines

㉑

⑬

p.24 ↓ to Yosemite Village

Happy Isles: Shaded by deep old-growth forest and hemmed in by soaring walls of bright granite, Happy Isles takes its name from a cluster of small islands in the Merced River. Gripped here between the cliffs of Grizzly Peak and the broad, bald apron of Glacier Point, the Merced dashes around the islands before coasting onto the flat floor of Yosemite Valley. Short trails loop throughout this refreshing site, criss-crossing the river and leading to a nature center, a distinctive wetlands area, and the site of a devastating 1996 rockfall. The site also serves as trailhead for the classic hike to Vernal and Nevada Falls.

Nature Center at Happy Isles: Geared to families, this small but engaging interpretive center profiles the forest ecosystems of Yosemite Valley. You'll find taxidermied examples of the valley's denizens, recordings of their calls, and samples of their footprints and scat. Here, too: a special exhibit on night animals, and a bark-and-leaf key for identifying the valley's trees.

Happy Isles Fen: To the west of the nature center, a boardwalk path crosses the Happy Isles Fen, a saturated opening in the forest dominated by ferns, sedges, nettles, and rushes. A "fen" is a type of wet meadow that has accumulated substantial amounts of partially decomposed plant matter, called "peat." Unlike bogs, fens receive nutrients in runoff from surrounding lands and are therefore richer in nutrients than bogs, which must rely on rainwater and snow for nutrients. In Happy Isles water percolates through neighboring talus fields and collects here. Thick layers of spongy peat have accumulated through the years, growing higher in the middle, shedding water outward, killing trees along the border, and expanding the fen.

Happy Isles Rockfall Exhibit: At 7 p.m. on July 10, 1996, huge slabs of granite released from the cliffs high above this point and fell to the ground. The slabs were about 30 feet thick, 900 feet long, and weighed a total of 68,000 tons. They slid down the upper cliffs, then went into free fall for 1,800 feet before slamming into the forest at about 270 mph. One person was killed, two severely injured, and the air blast snapped off 1,000 trees and created an enormous dust cloud. Signs describe the event in detail and identify the precise spot on the cliff where the slabs released.

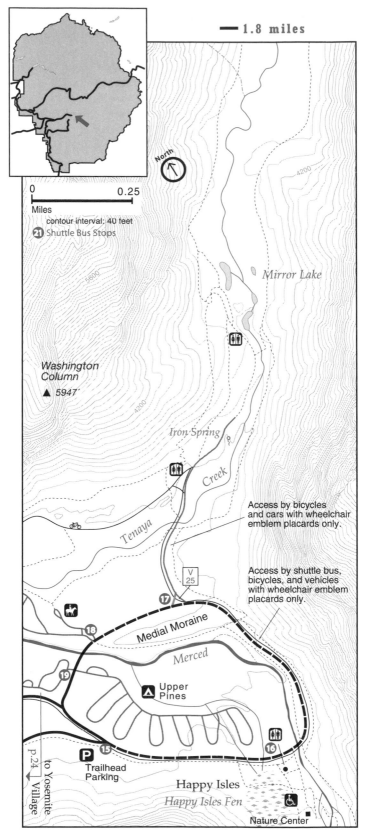

— **1.8 miles**

0   0.25

Miles

contour interval: 40 feet

21 Shuttle Bus Stops

Mirror Lake

Washington Column

▲ *5947'*

Iron Spring

Creek

Tenaya

Access by bicycles and cars with wheelchair emblem placards only.

Access by shuttle bus, bicycles, and vehicles with wheelchair emblem placards only.

V 25

17

18

Medial Moraine

Merced

19

▲ Upper Pines

15 P Trailhead Parking

16

to Yosemite Village

p.24

Happy Isles

Happy Isles Fen

Nature Center

Medial Moraine: As the road approaches shuttle stop #17 and the Mirror Lake Trailhead, it drops over a narrow, forested ridge that extends for a quarter mile to the west. Often identified as a medial moraine, it may have been formed in the late Pleistocene epoch from debris pushed together by two adjacent glaciers—one from Tenaya Canyon, the other from the upper Merced Canyon. Other geologists contend that it is a recessional moraine left by either the Tenaya Glacier or the Merced Glacier.

Mirror Lake: Best seen in spring and early summer when water levels are high, Mirror Lake formed after enormous boulders crashed down from nearby cliffs and dammed Tenaya Creek. Through the years, the lake became shallower and shallower as the creek carried down sediments from the high country and deposited them here. For many years, the park service excavated the lake each autumn, but since 1971 nature has been allowed to take its course. The former lake is now, at best, a pond surrounded by wet meadow and enlivened by the croaks of Pacific tree frogs.

Given time, the meadow will probably yield to forest. In the meantime, this relatively wide opening offers splendid vistas of Basket Dome, Mount Watkins, and Half Dome. Mirror Lake is a 1.0-mile walk from the trailhead. A rewarding 3.0-mile loop extends the outing through the lightly visited lower reaches of Tenaya Canyon.

Nature Note ▪ In the Mirror Lake area it is easy to see the track of the immense Ice Age glacier that carved out Tenaya Canyon. Its distinctive U-shaped profile can be traced along the facing granite walls of Basket Dome and Half Dome. ▪

An 1872 lithograph pictures hunters on Mirror Lake.

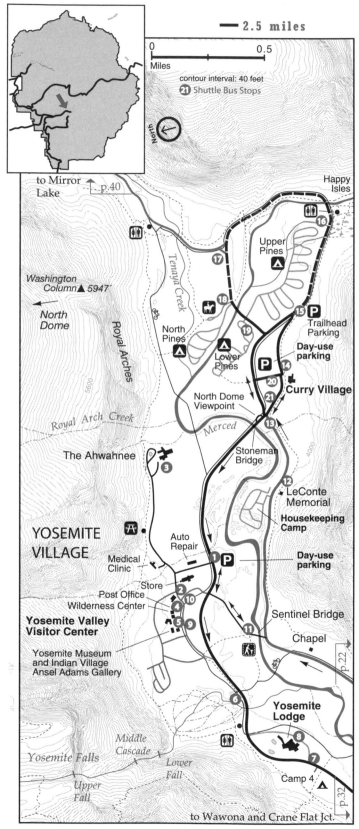

2.5 miles

0   0.5
Miles

contour interval: 40 feet
㉑ Shuttle Bus Stops

North

to Mirror Lake   p.40

Happy Isles

Upper Pines

Tenaya Creek

⑰

Washington Column ▲ 5947'

⑱

North Dome

⑮ P
Trailhead Parking

Day-use parking

North Pines

⑲

Lower Pines

Royal Arches

P ⑭

⑳

Curry Village

5600

North Dome Viewpoint

Royal Arch Creek

Merced

⑬

⑤ The Ahwahnee

③

Stoneman Bridge

⑫ LeConte Memorial

Housekeeping Camp

4000

YOSEMITE VILLAGE

Auto Repair

① P

Day-use parking

Medical Clinic

Store

Post Office

Wilderness Center

Yosemite Valley Visitor Center

②

④ ⑩

⑤ ⑨

Sentinel Bridge

⑪

Chapel

p.22

Yosemite Museum and Indian Village
Ansel Adams Gallery

⑥

Yosemite Lodge

Middle Cascade

⑧

Yosemite Falls

Lower Fall

⑦

Camp 4

Upper Fall

p.32

to Wawona and Crane Flat Jct.

North Dome and Royal Arches: This spot offers a classic vista across Stoneman Meadow to North Dome, which is poised over the concentric fracture lines of Royal Arches. Exfoliation created North Dome by gradually spalling concentric slabs of rock away from the granite mass. Exfoliation—perhaps aided by an undercutting glacier—also created Royal Arches, a series of recessed arches that rise as high as 1,000 feet and overhang the valley floor. To the right of the arches stands Washington Column, 1,500 feet high.

The Ahwahnee Hotel: Isolated from the hubbub of Yosemite Village and the valley's roads, The Ahwahnee's glass, timber, and stacked-stone facade stands beside a meadow at the base of Royal Arches. Designed by Gilbert Stanley Underwood and opened in 1927, the Ahwahnee still puts up affluent guests in high style—yet many of its common areas, including the Great Lounge, are open to non-paying guests. The building is a National Historic Landmark loaded with rustic period furnishings, hand-painted tapestries, Turkish rugs, and stained-glass windows.

Yosemite Village: The retail hub of the valley and site of several worthwhile interpretive stops, Yosemite Village lies at the mouth of Indian Canyon and within easy walking distance of Yosemite Falls.

Yosemite Valley Visitor Center: Located in the heart of the village, this bustling information center offers exhibits and videos on such topics as the role of fire in Yosemite, geology, bears, and common plants. Other displays describe the formation of marquee landmarks such as Half Dome, El Capitan, and the Three Brothers. The center also showcases John Muir, covers conservation history, and houses an excellent book store.

Yosemite Museum: This small museum adjacent to the visitor center mounts an impressive exhibit of basketry produced by the indigenous peoples of the valley and region, including the Ahwahneechee, Paiute, and Miwok. You'll also find obsidian points knapped by ancient Yosemite dwellers circa 2000 BC, buckskin clothing, and landscape paintings by Bierstadt, Moran, and other artists. Present-day local artisans often demonstrate traditional craft techniques.

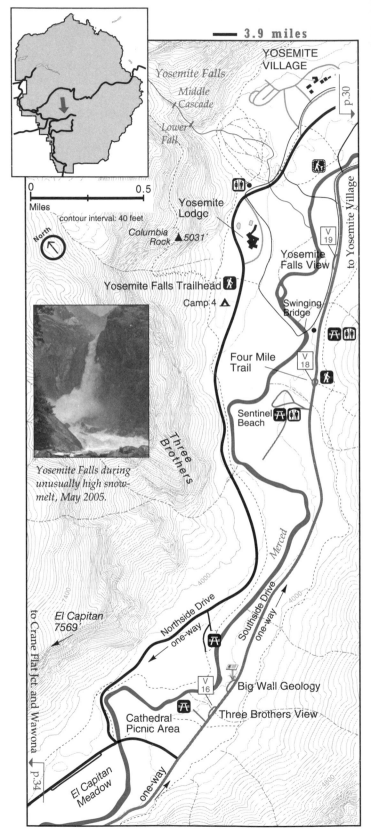

YOSEMITE VILLAGE

Yosemite Falls

Middle Cascade

Lower Fall

p.30

to Yosemite Village

Yosemite Lodge

Columbia Rock ▲5031'

V 19

Yosemite Falls View

Yosemite Falls Trailhead 🚶

Camp 4 ▲

Swinging Bridge

Four Mile Trail

V 18

Sentinel Beach

Three Brothers

Yosemite Falls during unusually high snow-melt, May 2005.

0   0.5

Miles

contour interval: 40 feet

North

Merced

Northside Drive one-way

Southside Drive one-way

El Capitan 7569'

to Crane Flat Jct. and Wawona

V 16

Big Wall Geology

Cathedral Picnic Area

Three Brothers View

p.34

El Capitan Meadow

one-way

32

Yosemite Falls: Tallest waterfall in the United States and fifth tallest in the world, Yosemite Falls plunges a total of 2,425 vertical feet in three spectacular steps: the Upper Fall (1,430 feet), Middle Cascade (675 feet), and Lower Fall (320 feet). Fed by rainwater and melted snow and ice, the falls thunder as a broad plume of white water in May, but they narrow in late summer to a reserved column of spray. John Muir once inched out to the brink of the Upper Fall along a ledge so narrow it accommodated just a portion of his heels. The view "down into the heart of the bright irised throng of comet-like streamers" was worth it, he stated, but he never did it again. The trail from the shuttle stop makes a leisurely 0.5-mile loop through the cedar-and-oak forest, spans several branches of Yosemite Creek, and offers fine vistas of Lower and Upper Yosemite Falls.

Camp 4 Sunnyside Campground: A gathering place for serious technical rock climbers, this campground beneath Eagle Peak (7,779 feet) offers a glimpse of the climber's life: mounds of clinking gear, nylon webbing, dainty shoes, and short rations. Notices on bulletin boards address intriguing sidelights of life on the big walls: the hazards of cliff-climbing bears and falling haul bags, locations of peregrine falcon nests, overnight etiquette, and tips for "vertical relief" while dangling a thousand feet off the ground.

The site is also the trailhead for Upper Yosemite Fall, a strenuous 7.2-mile round trip. Across the road, a different trail follows the banks of the Merced through Leidig Meadow to Swinging Bridge. The meadow offers an excellent view of Yosemite Falls.

El Capitan Meadow: A likely place to spot mule deer early or late in the day, El Capitan Meadow lies directly beneath the smooth and nearly vertical face of El Capitan and across the valley from Cathedral Rocks and Cathedral Spires. Here people sporting binoculars and spotting scopes are probably not watching birds, but rather climbers making their way up some of the most difficult routes in the park. In April and May, look for wild iris—floppy blossoms of blue, white, and yellow—intermingled with the meadow grasses. Great horned owls live among the oaks and incense cedars at the fringe of the meadow and hunt for rodents.

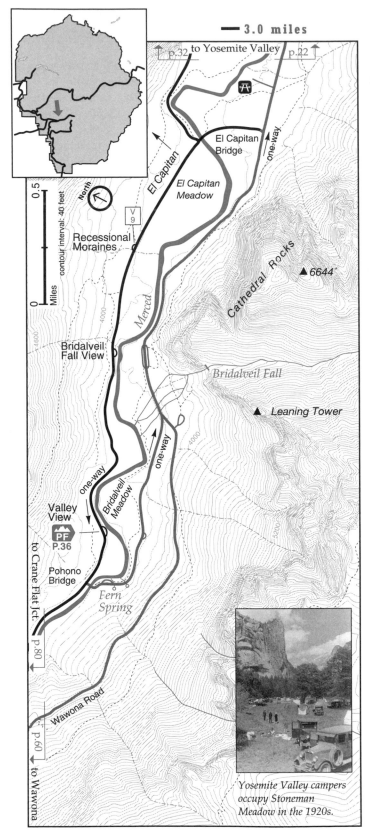

to Yosemite Valley
p.32   p.22

El Capitan Bridge

one-way

El Capitan

El Capitan Meadow

North

contour interval: 40 feet

V9

Recessional Moraines

Cathedral Rocks

▲ 6644

Merced

Miles

.5

0

4000

Bridalveil Fall View

Bridalveil Fall

▲ Leaning Tower

4000

one-way

5200

one-way

Bridalveil Meadow

Valley View

PF P.36

to Crane Flat Jct.

Pohono Bridge

Fern Spring

Wawona Road

p.80

p.60

to Wawona

Yosemite Valley campers occupy Stoneman Meadow in the 1920s.

El Capitan Moraine: A low ridge extends through the forest toward the Merced River and Cathedral Rocks. This deposit of glacial debris is a recessional moraine, left by the valley's last glacier about 16,000 years ago as it paused during its retreat. It once formed a dam across the valley, creating a shallow lake that extended about 5.5 miles to the east. The lake later filled in and became a marshy wetland. The dam was blasted in 1879 to lower the valley's water table and to reduce the mosquito population. The drier soil allowed incense cedar and ponderosa pine to invade the valley floor at the expense of wetland plants and black oaks.

Nature Note ■ California Black Oaks: Easily differentiated from other oaks by their pointy leaves, black oaks provided the Ahwahneechee with a plentiful source of nutritious food: acorns. Today deer, gray squirrels, band-tailed pigeons, and acorn woodpeckers depend on the black oak for food. Unfortunately, Yosemite Valley's black oaks are in decline due to unnatural causes. Healthy oaks need ample sunlight and loose soil. Soil compaction from human foot traffic has had a detrimental effect, and fire suppression has allowed other species of trees, such as ponderosa pines and incense cedars, to grow up around the oaks and shade them out. ■

Bridalveil Fall: Across the valley, Bridalveil Fall spills from its niche in the Cathedral Rocks. Bridalveil's hanging valley existed prior to glaciation, but glacial action lengthened the distance from brink to plunge pool by gouging out the valley floor and steepening the valley walls. At the onset of the Pleistocene, other tributaries of the Merced River were also entering the valley by way of steep cascades that began up to hundreds of feet above the valley floor in hanging valleys.

Pinkish gravels in the bed of the Merced River below this turnout have been carried here—mainly by glacial action—from sites roughly 18 miles west.

Valley View: Best seen in late afternoon or early evening as the sun glides westward, this classic vista of Yosemite Valley takes in El Capitan, Sentinel Rock, Cathedral Rocks, and Bridalveil Fall. Beneath them lies expansive Bridalveil Meadow just across the Merced River.

Valley View Panorama

El Capitan
7,569 feet

Merced
River

Half Dome
8,842 feet

Sentinel Rock

Cathedral Peaks

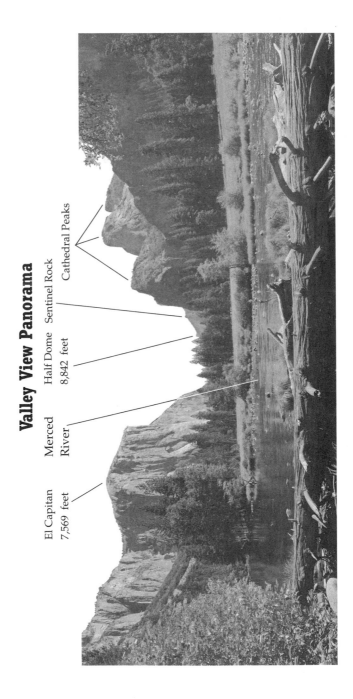

Reading the Landscape

■ Merced River ■ A tributary of the San Joaquin Valley watershed, the Merced River originates along the ragged crest of the Sierra Nevada and drains the southern portion of the park (about 450 square miles). Its upper section encompasses more than 1,000 small lakes and ponds, and many tributary streams—some of which begin at elevations of 13,000 feet. Here in the valley, the Merced cuts a shallow, meandering channel across a relatively flat bed of sediment and debris, much of which was deposited during the advance and retreat of a succession of glaciers. One of the last glaciers left a moraine near El Capitan that dammed the river and created a short-lived lake that was quickly succeeded by swampy meadows.

■ Flood of 1997 ■ Normally sedate during summer, the Merced River in spring flood can take on surprising force and volume. A sign at this turnout indicates the maximum water height here during the Flood of 1997—the result of a strange and historic January deluge. A torrential, three-day downpour followed by unseasonably warm weather bloated the Merced watershed with rain and meltwater. Yosemite Falls raged with such force that windows and walls rattled in the homes below. The river and streams jumped their banks and flooded the floor of the valley to depths of 10 feet in some places. Roughly 2,000 people were stranded, and the valley was closed to visitors for more than two months.

■ Bridalveil Meadow ■ Across the river, Bridalveil Meadow stretches beneath El Capitan, Cathedral Rocks, and Bridalveil Fall. While camped in this meadow during late March 1851, members of the Mariposa Battalion first applied the name Yosemite to the valley, in the mistaken belief that the Indians who inhabited the valley bore that name. They actually called themselves the Ahwahneechee. About 50 years later, John Muir and President Theodore Roosevelt camped in the same meadow and hatched a plan to greatly expand the boundaries of the park.

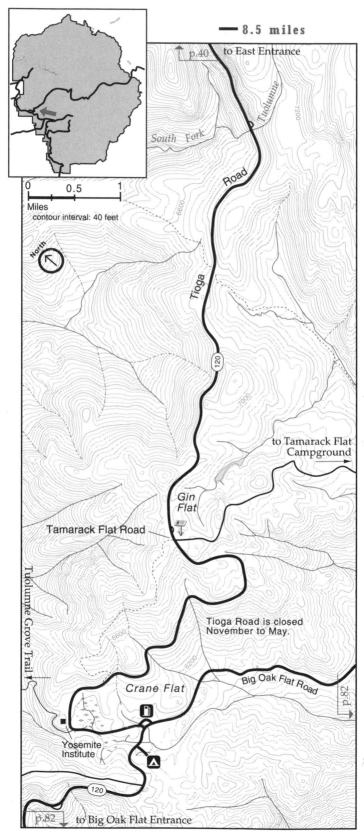

p.40 to East Entrance

8.5 miles

0   0.5   1
Miles
contour interval: 40 feet

North

South Fork

Tuolumne

Road

Tioga

120

to Tamarack Flat
Campground

Gin
Flat

Tamarack Flat Road

Tioga Road is closed
November to May.

Big Oak Flat Road

p.82

Tuolumne Grove Trail

Crane Flat

Yosemite
Institute

120

p.82 to Big Oak Flat Entrance

38

Tioga Road

Tamarack Flat Road: Narrow, rough, and winding, this quiet 3-mile side road leads through mixed conifer forest. Although a large area burned recently, it is now bursting with tall saplings and big leaf lupine. The road, once a section of the Old Big Oak Flat Road, ends at a campground located among large knobs of weathered granite.

Gin Flat and the Historic Tioga Road: A sign here describes the harrowing travel conditions that existed along the Old Tioga Road, which wound through the forest north of the present road. Gin Flat, elevation 7,036 feet, sports masses of purple Bridge's gilia in June, yampah in July, and meadow goldenrod in August. The huge tree beside the road is a Jeffrey pine.

Tuolumne Grove: One of Yosemite's three groves of giant sequoia trees, Tuolumne Grove consists of 25 scattered giants that dwarf the mature trees growing beside them: sugar pines, Jeffrey pines, white firs, and incense cedars. Massive, fire resistant, and cloaked with thick, reddish brown bark, the sequoia is the largest, non-clonal living thing on Earth. It also ranks as one of the fastest growing and longest living species. The oldest sequoia on record (not a Yosemite tree) reached a documented age of 3,200 years. The trail to the grove (a 2.5-mile round trip with a 500-foot elevation change) descends through mixed conifer forest along an 1870s carriage road. Once in the grove, a short interpretive trail loops among the giant trunks.

Crane Flat: This lush mid-elevation meadow, or "flat," meanders through the surrounding forest and occasionally approaches Tioga Road between the Crane Flat gas station and the Yosemite Institute. Its moist lower end supports a vibrant crush of wetland flowers such as Sierra rein orchids, bistorts, shooting stars, wild geraniums, monkey flowers, and masses of tall, yellow, California coneflowers. A very different plant community lives in Crane Flat's drier upper end: broadleaf lupines, forget-me-nots, ranger buttons, and stands of corn lilies. At an elevation of roughly 6,200 feet, Crane Flat lies at the upper margin of the mixed conifer forest, which includes incense cedar, black oak, Douglas fir, Jeffrey pine, sugar pine, and ponderosa pine.

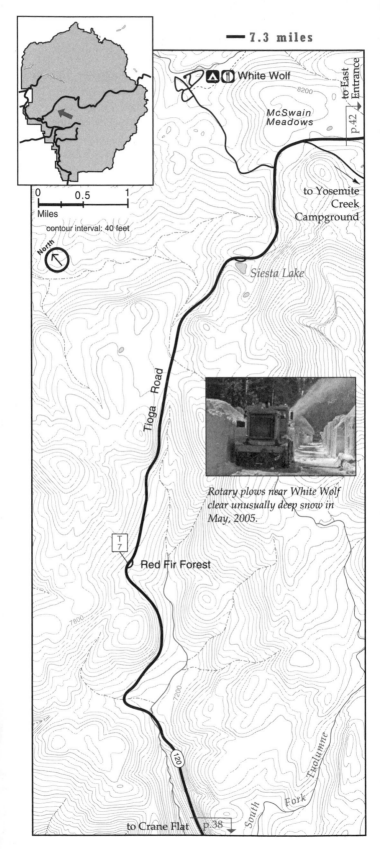

White Wolf

McSwain Meadows

8200

p.42
to East Entrance

to Yosemite Creek Campground

Siesta Lake

Tioga Road

Rotary plows near White Wolf clear unusually deep snow in May, 2005.

T 7

Red Fir Forest

7800

7200

120

South Fork Tuolumne

to Crane Flat p.38

Miles

0   0.5   1

contour interval: 40 feet

North

White Wolf: Another opportunity to exit busy Tioga Road, the White Wolf area takes in a small, moist meadow amid the lodgepole pine/red fir forest. In the meadow, look for meadow penstemon (deep blue to purple) and bull elephanthead (pink). Coyotes, mule deer, and black bear roam the surrounding forest. Cassin's finches, sparrow-sized with a plush red crown, warble and flit among the trees. White Wolf is a High Sierra Camp with neat white cottages, wall tents, a campground, and restaurant.

Yosemite Creek Campground: The rugged side road down to Yosemite Creek Campground follows the jarring course of the Old Tioga Road. Completed in 1883 as a wagon route to supply the Tioga Mine near Tioga Pass, the road offered the only motor route across the park until 1961. Portions of the old road bed now form hiking trails in various parts of the park, including Tuolumne Meadows.

Siesta Lake: Surrounded by lodgepole pines, this small, shallow lake dotted with pond lilies is in the latter stages of eutrophication—the gradual filling in with decomposed plant material that will eventually lead to the formation of a meadow. In the meantime, it provides a rich aquatic environment for a variety of insects and amphibians, including the Pacific tree frog.

　　The lake formed behind a morainal dam, part of which is visible across the road. The glacier responsible for the moraine coalesced along the crest of the ridge south of the lake. Along the shore of the lake, look for asters, Brewer's lupine, broadleaf lupine, and sulphur flowers.

Red Fir Forest: This turnout faces a nearly pure stand of California red fir. Prominent among a forest of evergreens, the red fir grows tall, straight, and slender with rough, reddish brown bark and few if any branches for some distance up its trunk. It thrives on moisture from heavy snows that accumulate in Yosemite at elevations between 7,000 and 8,000 feet, but it is also found outside that range. The red fir grows in the company of lodgepole pine, western juniper, western white pine, sugar pine, and white fir.

　　Pine martens, a rarely seen member of the weasel family, live in these forests and prey on squirrels and other small rodents.

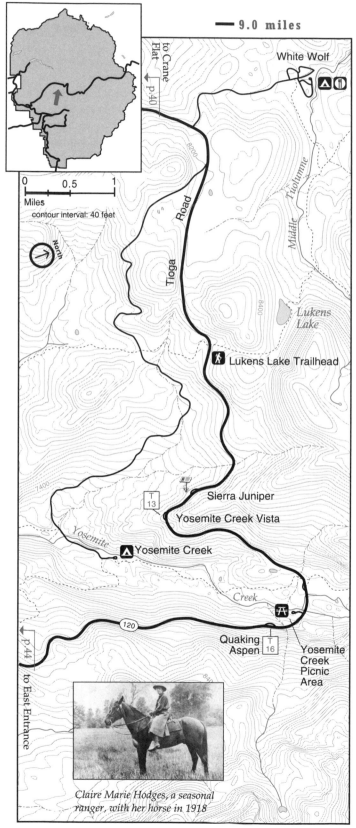

9.0 miles

to Crane Flat
p 40

White Wolf

Tioga Road

8200

Lukens Lake

8400

Lukens Lake Trailhead

Tuolumne

Middle

7400

Sierra Juniper

T 13

Yosemite Creek Vista

Yosemite

Yosemite Creek

Creek

120

Quaking Aspen
T 16

Yosemite Creek Picnic Area

8400

to East Entrance
p 44

North

0   0.5   1
Miles
contour interval: 40 feet

Claire Marie Hodges, a seasonal ranger, with her horse in 1918

Lukens Lake Trail: This easy hike (1.6 miles round trip) starts on the north side of the road and leads through dense red fir forest to Lukens Lake, a small, shallow, relatively warm lake popular with families as a swimming and picnic site. Lush wildflower meadows border the nine-acre lake on two sides, one of them thick with corn lilies. Along the way, look for Williamson's sapsuckers and black-backed woodpeckers tapping tree trunks for insects. Beyond this trailhead, the road emerges from the forest and bounds through more open country with plenty of vistas of canyons, granite domes, and bare-rock peaks.

Sierra Juniper: This isolated Sierra juniper overlooks the Yosemite Creek drainage and grows across the road from a fine example in cross-section of the parallel concentric joints that underlie the rounded surface of Yosemite's granite domes and that play such a leading role in the exfoliation process. Sierra junipers are hardy, drought tolerant, and long lived. Some in the Yosemite area are thought to be 2,000 years old. Intolerant of shade, they thrive in dry open country, often where no other tree can survive. The juniper depends on animals, mostly birds, to disperse seed contained in the tree's small, bluish fruits. These seeds do not germinate well unless they pass through the digestive tract of an animal.

Yosemite Creek Vista: This pleasing, south-facing point offers the chance to get out and amble around on a broad shoulder of bright granite. Sierra junipers and Jeffrey pines grow from cracks in the rock and provide welcome pools of shade. With luck, you might spot a northern alligator lizard—a speckled, eight-inch reptile that adapts to high elevation by operating at a lower body temperature than most lizards and by retaining its eggs until the young are hatched.

Yosemite Creek Picnic Area: Yosemite Creek, a modest brook at this point in late summer, threads its way among large boulders and passes through a small glen shaded by evergreens and enlivened by bouquets of scarlet penstemon. Seven miles downstream, after gathering more force from tributaries, Yosemite Creek plunges 2,425 feet into Yosemite Valley as Yosemite Falls.

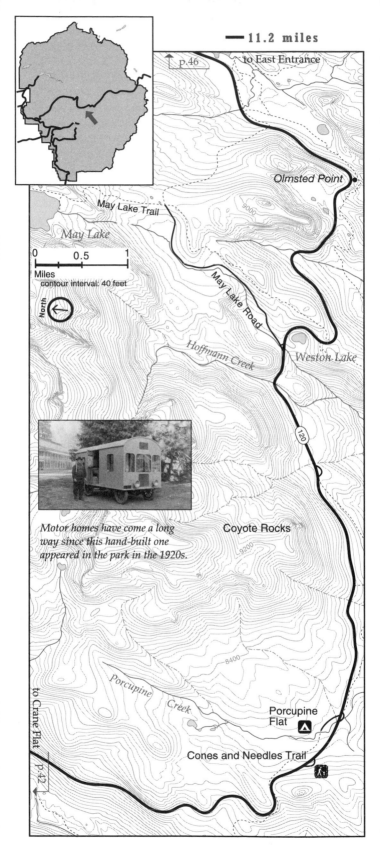

p.46

to East Entrance

Olmsted Point

May Lake Trail

May Lake

9000

May Lake Road

Hoffmann Creek

Weston Lake

0   0.5   1

Miles
contour interval: 40 feet

North

120

Motor homes have come a long
way since this hand-built one
appeared in the park in the 1920s.

Coyote Rocks

9200

8400

Porcupine Creek

to Crane Flat
p.42

Porcupine
Flat

Cones and Needles Trail

Weston Lake: Known informally as Weston Lake, after the photographer Edward Weston, this shallow body of water studded with boulders offers a refuge from Tioga Road traffic and a chance to admire the white blossoms of Labrador tea, a heath shrub two to five feet high, that grows in profusion along the shore.

May Lake Trail: This rewarding hike (2.4-mile round trip; 400-foot elevation gain) ambles through a classic High Sierra landscape of scattered stands of trees, big weathered boulders, vast ramps of gray-white granite, and boundless vistas of the Sierra crest. May Lake, site of a High Sierra Camp, is a tarn—a small lake basin carved out by a glacier on Mount Hoffmann.

May Lake Road: This worthwhile side road runs north 1.8 miles to the trailhead for May Lake, a deservedly popular day hike. Along the way, the road meanders under the gleaming granite slopes of Mount Hoffmann and flanks a lovely, boulder-studded meadow named Snow Flat, where more snow gathers and lasts longer than almost anywhere else in Yosemite. The result is often a late bloom of wildflowers.

At the trailhead, check out the small pond; its clear water has been made brown by tannic acid from surrounding pines, and its relatively warm waters wriggle with thousands of large tadpoles. Some of these are juvenile mountain yellow-legged frogs, an unusual species that spends two to four years as a tadpole before metamorphosing. Once common in the High Sierra, it has disappeared from much of its former range.

Cones and Needles Trail: Signs along this short trail identify living specimens of the five tree species that characterize Yosemite forests at this elevation. Called the lodgepole pine/red fir forest, these woodlands also include white fir, western white pine, and Jeffrey pine—sometimes very difficult to distinguish from ponderosa pine. In autumn, Clark's nutcrackers use their long bills to pry open the cones of Jeffrey pines; they may cache up to 30,000 seeds in scattered sites as a winter food source. Many of the seeds go uneaten, though, so the nutcracker's efforts serve as a reproductive aid for Jeffrey pines. Underfoot, look for mats of Brewer's lupine, one of 60 lupine species in the park.

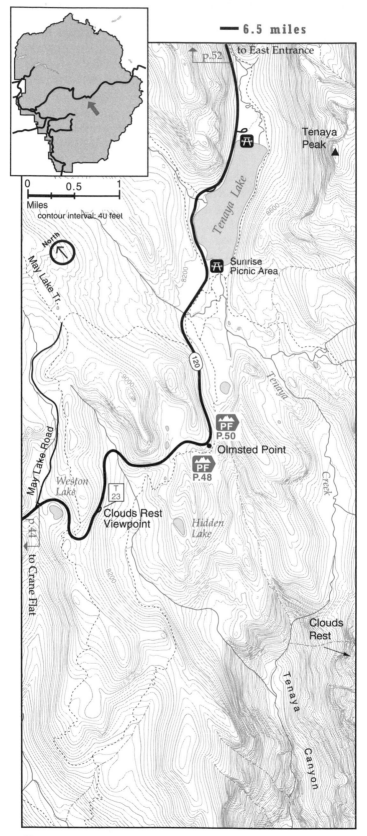

p.52 to East Entrance

— 6.5 miles

Tenaya Peak

Tenaya Lake

p.52 to East Entrance

0   0.5   1
Miles
contour interval: 4U feet

North

May Lake Tr.

8200

8600

Sunrise Picnic Area

120

May Lake Road

Tenaya

9000

PF
P.50
Olmsted Point

PF
P.48

Weston Lake

T 23

Clouds Rest Viewpoint

Hidden Lake

Creek

p.41 to Crane Flat

8200

Clouds Rest

Tenaya

Tenaya Canyon

46

Olmsted Point: This exposed promontory of gently sloping granite offers two of the best vistas in Yosemite. To the southwest, the view takes in Clouds Rest, Half Dome, Mount Watkins, and portions of glacially carved Tenaya Canyon. To the northeast, it looks up the canyon to Tenaya Lake and brings into clear perspective the U-shaped granite cradle occupied by the lake.

Over the parking lot stands a low knob of granite, criss-crossed with parallel joints and studded with isolated boulders carried to this point and then abandoned by retreating glaciers. Below and to the right, water drains across the open rock slope from aptly named Hidden Lake, which is obscured by a pocket of lodgepole pine.

To leave the bulk of the crowd behind, take the short trail that drops left from the edge of the parking lot. It traverses the flank of Olmsted Point and leads to a definitive vista of Tenaya Canyon's southeast wall— a continuous ridge of granite extending from Clouds Rest to Half Dome, which looks almost like a fin from this perspective. Along the way, several banner trees grow from cracks in the rock, including a marvelous western juniper near the trailhead.

The best vantage point to view Tenaya Lake is at the northeast end of the parking area.

Clouds Rest: The massive slope of scalloped granite that rises high above the evergreen forest to the south is a peak called Clouds Rest, elevation 9,926 feet, so named for its tendency to gather clouds near its summit. Nearly barren of trees, its exfoliated cliffs plunge into Tenaya Canyon. The singular dome beyond is Mount Starr King, 9,092 feet. The forest below this turnoff bears evidence of the increasingly brutal effects of high-elevation weather: wind-blasted "banner" trees capable of growing branches only on the downwind side of the trunk.

Nature Note ■ Mountain Pocket Gophers: Among the most specialized of North American burrowing mammals, these thick-set, short-necked, small to medium-sized rodents have large, external cheek pouches lined with fur, the "pockets" that give them their name. They use these pouches to gather food or bedding material for nests, and empty them by turning them inside out. Their burrows are commonly spotted in meadows at this elevation in spring. ■

Half Dome from Olmsted Point

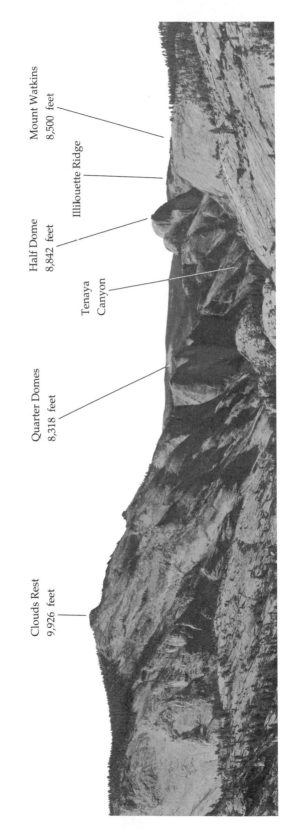

Clouds Rest
9,926 feet

Quarter Domes
8,318 feet

Tenaya
Canyon

Half Dome
8,842 feet

Illilouette Ridge

Mount Watkins
8,500 feet

Reading the Landscape

■ **Tenaya Canyon** ■ A classic, glacially carved valley, Tenaya Canyon drops away from Olmsted Point for nearly 2,000 vertical feet. Prior to the ice ages, Tenaya Canyon was a narrow, V-shaped valley eroded by Tenaya Creek. But no erosive force can match the power of glacial ice. Armed with abrasive rock fragments plucked and scoured from the bedrock, the succession of glaciers that moved through Tenaya Canyon widened, deepened, and straightened the existing valley into the capacious, U-shaped half-pipe we see today.

■ **Glacial Polish** ■ While ambling around Olmsted Point, take note of the rock surface underfoot. Here and there, one comes across patches of granite as smooth as a headstone. These patches are remnants of larger surfaces polished by Ice Age glaciers. In these places, the moving ice pressed fine-grained sediment against the rock, buffing the surface smooth. When viewed closely, the polished areas often bear fine, parallel scratches that indicate which direction the ice moved.

■ **Glacial Erratics** ■ Many of the boulders strewn across the surface of Olmsted Point are glacial erratics. That is, they were picked up elsewhere by glaciers, embedded in the moving ice, and transported to this point, where they were left behind after the ice melted. Some of the most obvious examples litter the high knob of rock to the right of the parking area.

■ **Yellow-bellied Marmots** ■ Often seen around Olmsted Point, these western relatives of the woodchuck live in dens on hillsides, under rock piles, or in crevices and other rocky shelters. When alarmed, they retreat to the entrances of their dens and chirp or whistle. They eat nothing but green vegetation and put on a layer of fat sufficient to see them through the winter. True hibernators, marmots den up for the winter as early as August and can remain in hibernation through February or March. During this time, their body temperatures plunge from 95 degrees to the low 40s; heart rates drop from 100 beats per minute to 15; and oxygen consumption falls to just one-tenth the normal rate. Even so, marmots lose from 30 to 50 percent of their body weight during winter.

Tenaya lake from Olmsted Point

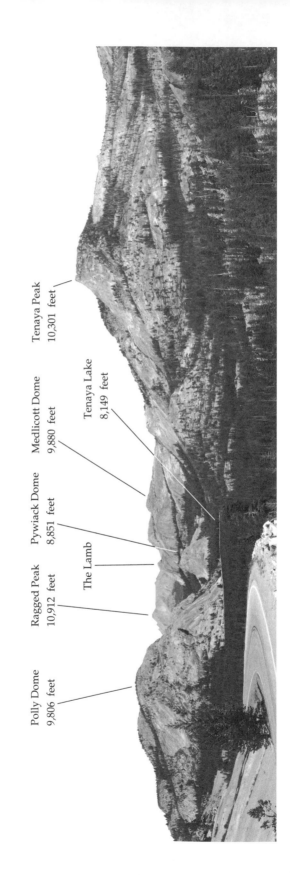

Polly Dome
9,806 feet

Ragged Peak
10,912 feet

The Lamb

Pywiack Dome
8,851 feet

Medlicott Dome
9,880 feet

Tenaya Lake
8,149 feet

Tenaya Peak
10,301 feet

Reading the Landscape

■ Polly Dome ■ Bulking 1,600 feet above Tenaya Lake's northeastern shore, Polly Dome bears an elongated shape which, like so many of the park's landmarks, is governed by the orientation of fractures, or joints, within the granite. In this case, the joints are long and straight, lending a rectangular character to the dome when seen from overhead. It also contains parallel concentric joints, vital to the exfoliation process that accounts for the dome's rounded appearance.

Look for the clear, glacial footprint that has been left between Polly Dome's southern flank and the lower slopes of Tenaya Peak. The broad, U-shaped profile bends slightly to the north, tracing the path of a massive lobe of glacial ice.

■ Pywiack Dome ■ Diminutive from this distance, Pywiack Dome takes its name from the Ahwahneechee name for Tenaya Lake: "Lake of the Glistening Rocks." The "glistening" refers to the glacial polish left on rock slopes surrounding the lake by passing glaciers. The immense weight of the ice, combined with fine rock particles, buffed the rock to a bright sheen in many places.

■ Tenaya Lake ■ Named for the mid-19th century leader of the Ahwahneechee people, Tenaya Lake is the site where the Mariposa Battalion surprised the Ahwahneechee in early June of 1851 and forced their surrender. The band was then taken to a reservation in California's Central Valley near Fresno. Later, the Ahwahneechee dispersed and joined bands of Paiute at Mono Lake and Miwok along the Tuolumne River.

■ Pikas ■ Common among the rocks of Olmsted Point, pikas are more often heard than seen. Their high, nasal bleats cut the air of the high country, especially in talus slopes near meadows. Closely related to rabbits and hares, pikas are about the size of hamsters, have small round ears, non-jumping hind legs, and no visible tails. Unlike marmots and ground squirrels, pikas remain active during winter, feeding off cached stacks of plants that they have cut and cured during the summer. Stacks of pika "hay" often contain as much as a bushel of grasses and sedges, thistles, stonecrop, and fireweed.

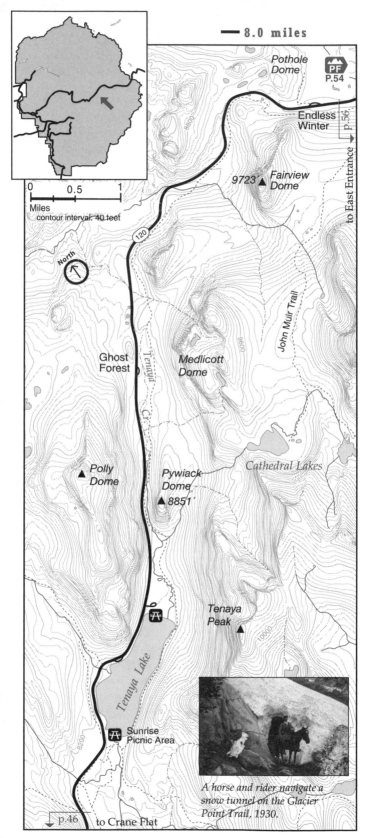

0   0.5   1

Miles
contour interval: 40 feet

North

PF P.54

Pothole
Dome

Endless
Winter

p.56

9723´ ▲ Fairview
Dome

to East Entrance

120

John Muir Trail

Ghost
Forest

Tenaya Cr.

Medlicott
Dome

9600

8800

Cathedral Lakes

Polly
▲ Dome

Pywiack
Dome
▲ 8851´

Tenaya
Peak ▲

10000

8200

Tenaya Lake

Sunrise
Picnic Area

A horse and rider navigate a
snow tunnel on the Glacier
Point Trail, 1930.

p.46 to Crane Flat

Tuolumne Meadows: The largest subalpine meadow in the Sierra Nevada, Tuolumne Meadows rambles along the Tuolumne River for about eight miles, offering grand vistas of surrounding domes and mountains. Laced with footpaths and crammed with wildflowers, the meadows form a rough dogleg that jogs north at the base of Pothole Dome. Subalpine tree species border the meadow on all sides.

Endless Winter: Located at the west end of Tuolumne Meadows, this turnout describes winter conditions in Yosemite's high country. In a typical year, roughly 12 feet of snow accumulates here. Extreme temperatures and a short growing season require plants and animals to adapt in fascinating ways.

Ghost Forest: This stand of mature lodgepoles grew in place of a "ghost forest" of silvery snags killed during the early 1900s by an infestation of needleminer moths. Needleminer larvae bore into the needles of lodgepole pine for food and shelter. If they occupy a tree in sufficient numbers, they can defoliate it and eventually kill it. Like wildfire, needleminer epidemics open up the forest canopy, encouraging the growth of young, sun-loving trees and shrubs.

Tenaya Lake: Nearly a mile long, 180 feet deep, and cradled by white-domed mountain slopes, Tenaya Lake formed in a bedrock basin carved out by the Tenaya branch of the great Tuolumne Glacier, which emerged along the Sierra crest during the Pleistocene. Its surface lies at an elevation of 8,150 feet.

Stumps of ancient trees protruding from the surface of Tenaya Lake offer stark evidence of severe droughts around AD 1100 and AD 1350. The trees grew when water levels were at least 70 feet lower than present. Scientists estimate that the first drought lasted 130 years; the second, at least 100.

Sunrise: A popular picnic area along the boulder-studded southwest shore of Tenaya Lake, Sunrise is protected from prevailing winds and provides fine vistas of Polly Dome, which looms 1,600 feet over the opposite end of the lake. It also acts as trailhead for Sunrise Lakes, a trio of small lakes tucked into the mountains to the south (7.5-mile round trip; 1,100-foot elevation gain). Here, too, a trail takes off along the south shore.

Tuolumne Meadows from Pothole Dome

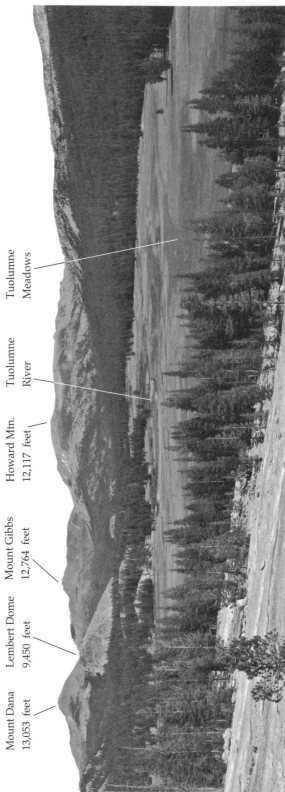

Mount Dana
13,053 feet

Lembert Dome
9,450 feet

Mount Gibbs
12,764 feet

Howard Mtn.
12,117 feet

Tuolumne
River

Tuolumne
Meadows

Reading the Landscape

■ Tuolumne Meadows ■ This expansive series of openings in the lodgepole pine forest extend along the Tuolumne River for roughly 8 to 10 miles. The meadows lie atop shallow depressions in the bedrock, which collect and retain moisture from snowmelt for much of the summer. The wet soils make it difficult for trees to establish themselves except along the fringes.

■ Subalpine Meadows ■ At 8,600 feet of elevation, the meadows fall solidly within the park's Subalpine Life Zone, where plants and animals must contend with an unforgivingly harsh climate, one that brings a much colder, much longer, and much snowier winter than Yosemite Valley experiences. Tuolumne Meadows often lie buried in as much as 10 to 12 feet of snow for half the year, and winter usually lasts for roughly eight months. The long winter makes for a short growing season, which in turn forces many subalpine plants and animals to accelerate their food-gathering and reproductive activities.

■ Lodgepole Pine ■ The predominant tree species in the forests surrounding Tuolumne Meadows is the lodgepole pine, a short-lived, sun-loving species that often pioneers areas burned by forest fires. During fires, heat opens the lodgepole's cones and disperses the seeds, but the species also reproduces very well without fire. This is especially true in areas like the Sierra, where summer sunshine is intense enough to melt the resin that binds the cones together.

■ Belding's Ground Squirrel ■ One of the most commonly seen animals in Tuolumne Meadows, Belding's ground squirrels have one of the longest hibernation periods of any North American animal: seven to eight months. During the short summer, they nearly double their body weight by eating many different plants and insects and enter hibernation as soon as they have enough stored fat to last the winter. Even so, many squirrels do not survive the winter. Some 50 percent to 90 percent of juveniles and 20 percent to 70 percent of adults die during hibernation. When they emerge in spring, females are reproductively receptive for just three to six hours. Competition among males for mates is so fierce that almost all males in a colony are injured—and some killed—in battles over females.

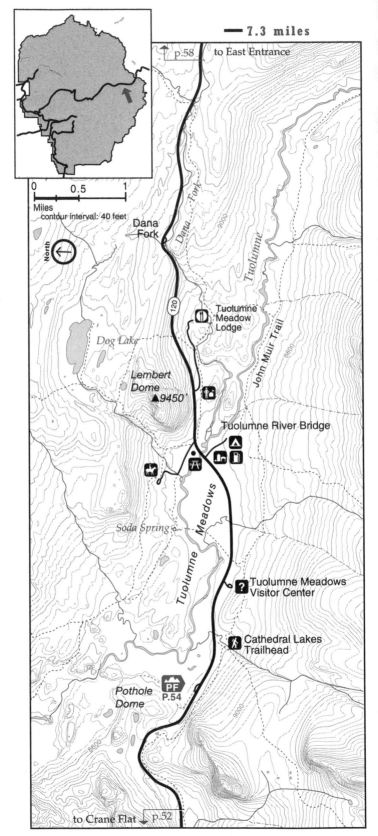

to East Entrance

p.58

Dana Fork

Dana Fork

Tuolumne

120

Tuolumne Meadow Lodge

Dog Lake

John Muir Trail

Lembert Dome

▲9450

Tuolumne River Bridge

Tuolumne Meadows

Soda Spring

Tuolumne Meadows Visitor Center

Cathedral Lakes Trailhead

Pothole Dome

PF
P.54

to Crane Flat
p.52

0   0.5   1
Miles
contour interval: 40 feet

North

Lembert Dome: Like Pothole Dome to the west but much larger, Lembert Dome is a *roche moutonnee.* Its west end serves as a trailhead for two popular day hikes. The first curves around the west and north sides of Lembert Dome and climbs to its summit for a knockout vista of Tuolumne Meadows and the surrounding peaks (4.0-mile round trip; 900-foot elevation gain). The second, to Soda Springs, is an easy 1.5-mile round-trip ramble through the meadows to a curious mineral spring and Parson's Lodge, a memorial honoring an early member of the Sierra Club.

Tuolumne River Bridge: The Tuolumne River officially begins just a few hundred yards upstream of this point, where the Dana Fork and Lyle Fork of the Tuolumne River come together. Fed mainly by snowmelt, the river flows west across Yosemite's northern wilderness to Hetch Hetchy Reservoir.

Tuolumne Meadows Visitor Center: Small but useful, this center houses a well-stocked bookstore, posts a schedule for ranger walks and other interpretive activities, and displays pressed specimens of some of the area's most common wildflowers.

Cathedral Lakes Trail: This 8.0-mile round-trip hike climbs 1,000 feet to a pair of shallow lakes nestled beneath the needle-like crest of Cathedral Peak, elevation 10,940 feet. Also visible from Tuolumne Meadows, the summit of Cathedral Peak protruded from the deepest glacial ice during the Pleistocene.

Pothole Dome: This pale brow of granite rises just 200 feet above a lush carpet of wildflowers and sedges at the west end of Tuolumne Meadows. During the ice ages, glaciers completely overrode this dome. Moving east to west, the ice wore down the dome's leading edge and steepened its "downstream" side by plucking rocks from its cliffs. Called a roche moutonnee, Pothole has a corresponding feature of the same type at the east end of the meadow—Lembert Dome.

It takes just 20 minutes to reach the top of Pothole Dome by way of a trail that skirts the fragile west end of the meadow. Few of Yosemite's footpaths offer so much for so little effort: sweeping vistas of the meadow, river, and surrounding peaks, and excellent examples of glacial polishing, striation, and glacial erratics.

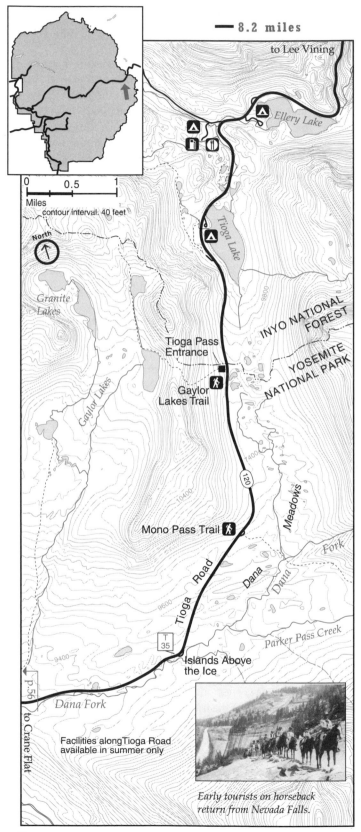

8.2 miles

to Lee Vining

Ellery Lake

Tioga Lake

INYO NATIONAL FOREST

YOSEMITE NATIONAL PARK

Tioga Pass Entrance

Gaylor Lakes Trail

Granite Lakes

Gaylor Lakes

North

contour interval: 40 feet

Mono Pass Trail

Tioga Road

120

Meadows

Dana Fork

Dana

Parker Pass Creek

T 35

Islands Above the Ice

to Crane Flat

Dana Fork

Facilities along Tioga Road available in summer only

Early tourists on horseback return from Nevada Falls.

58

Gaylor Lakes Trail: A spectacular day hike, this trail starts just west of the Tioga Pass Entrance Station and climbs into an expansive subalpine terrain graced by a cluster of high-elevation lakes at the very crest of the Sierra Nevada. Wildflowers abound, as do yellow-bellied marmots and Belding's ground squirrels. It's just a mile to the first lake. A longer trip that takes in all the lakes and visits nearby Granite Lakes requires a 6-mile, round-trip romp with an elevation gain of 1,000 feet.

Mono Pass Trail: This 8-mile round trip climbs 1,000 feet along an ancient trade route, passes old mining cabins, and tops out at Mono Pass, elevation 10,064 feet, which offers splendid vistas of Mount Gibbs, the Kuna Crest, and Mono Lake.

Dana Meadows: Another sprawling subalpine meadow, Dana Meadows is similar to Tuolumne Meadows but lies about 1,000 feet higher as is evident in the appearance of many of the trees, which are stunted and deformed. During the Pleistocene, a branch of the great Tuolumne Glacier formed in the mountains above the meadows and coalesced with another branch that formed above Lyell Canyon on the far side of the Kuna Crest.

Islands Above the Ice: This turnout offers a fine view to the east of Mount Dana, elevation 13,053 feet, and Mount Gibbs, elevation 12,764 feet. Both loom over the rushing waters of the Dana Fork. Here at the upper margin of the subalpine forest, thickets of dwarfed and deformed lodgepole pines, known as krummholtz, grow as a patchwork across otherwise open terrain. This is rich wildflower country that also supports 6- to 12-inch specimens of big sagebrush.

During Pleistocene glaciations, this area lay buried beneath as much as a thousand feet of slowly moving ice. To the west, several peaks—Cockscomb, Unicorn, and Cathedral—protruded from the glaciers as "islands above the ice," or nunataks.

Dana Fork Tuolumne River: The road parallels the Dana Fork through open forest of lodgepole pine. In mid-summer, lupine and asters brighten up the forest floor, and the stream slips over a bed of smooth granite slabs and gravel.

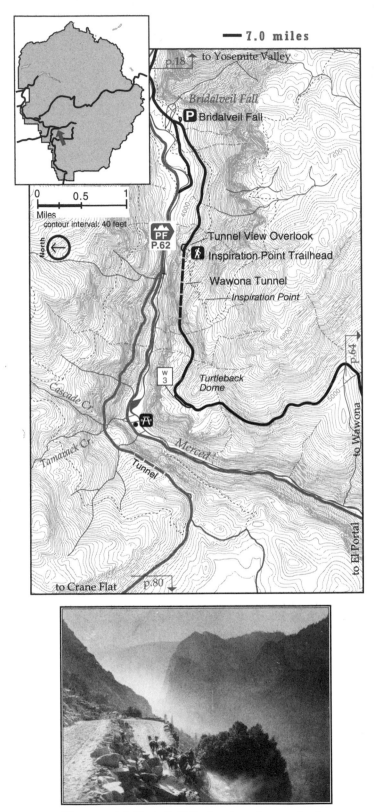

to Yosemite Valley
p.18

Bridalveil Fall

P Bridalveil Fall

7200

0   0.5   1

Miles
contour interval: 40 feet

North

4000

PF
P.62

Tunnel View Overlook

Inspiration Point Trailhead

Wawona Tunnel

Inspiration Point

6000

W
3

Turtleback Dome

Cascade Cr.

5000

to Wawona

p.64

Tamarack Cr.

Merced

Tunnel

to El Portal

to Crane Flat   p.80

*The approach to Yosemite Valley has always been spectacular.
Today's roads are wider and far less dusty.*

Wawona Road

Bridalveil Fall: The vista point for Bridalveil Fall lies a mere 2,000 feet from this major parking area, which usually is filled to capacity by mid-morning. The trail leads through a forest of incense cedar, oak, and ponderosa pine and connects with the rest of the valley's trail system.

Tunnel View Overlook: Located at the downhill mouth of Wawona Tunnel, this classic vista of the Yosemite Valley trench takes in El Capitan, Half Dome, Cathedral Rocks, and Bridalveil Fall. Immortalized by Ansel Adams's photograph, "Clearing Winter Storm," and often called the most photographed scene on Earth, the view draws thousands of visitors every day during summer.

Inspiration Point Trail: Across the highway from Tunnel View, this fairly steep trail climbs steadily away from the throngs to a granite promontory along the rim of the valley (2.6-mile round trip; 1,000-foot elevation gain). Often deserted, Inspiration Point offers an even more comprehensive panorama of Yosemite Valley than Tunnel View. Along the way, the trail passes through pockets of oaks, pines, and incense cedars, as well as thickets of manzanita. This is good terrain for ringtails—agile, cat-like relatives of the raccoon that ambush small rodents, lizards, snakes, and other prey at night.

Turtleback Dome: Here, the highway makes a broad, southerly curve around the open flanks of Turtleback Dome and offers a last glimpse of Yosemite Valley for southbound visitors.

The roadcut on the south side of the highway exposes concentric joints that underlie the surface of the dome and play a key role in exfoliation, a form of weathering that characterizes many of Yosemite's landmarks. The joints formed long ago when vertical pressure from the mass of overlying rock was released by erosion. The joints separate relatively thin layers of rock that spall or break loose in concentric shells. This concentric pattern develops in massive granites largely devoid of vertical jointing.

High above the road on the rounded upper surface of the dome stands a giant boulder. It is a glacial erratic, placed there by moving ice during Pleistocene glaciation.

Yosemite Valley from Tunnel View

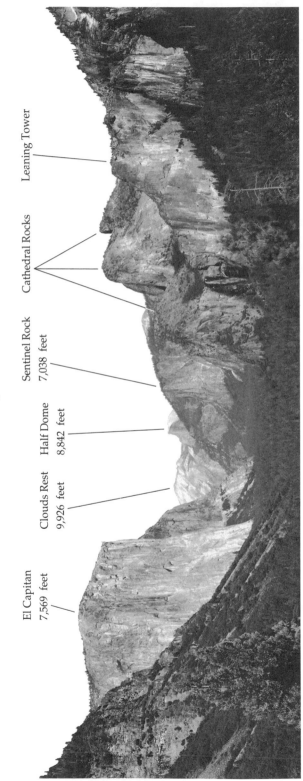

El Capitan
7,569 feet

Clouds Rest
9,926 feet

Half Dome
8,842 feet

Sentinel Rock
7,038 feet

Cathedral Rocks

Leaning Tower

Reading the Landscape

■ **El Capitan** ■ This renowned block of massive, virtually unjointed granite rises 3,206 feet above the valley floor. Composed of a type of granite that is exceptionally resistant to weathering and erosion, El Capitan massif also contains intrusions of diorite and pegmatite. It is one of the few landmarks in Yosemite Valley that was not entirely buried by moving ice during the most severe of the glacial advances. Its sheer, relatively smooth surfaces have posed a challenge to technical rock climbers for generations. John Muir observed that many consider it "the most sublime feature of the valley" and said it is "unrivaled in height and breadth and flawless strength."

■ **Clouds Rest** ■ Beyond and to the left of Half Dome, Clouds Rest stands as a high bank of granite along the southeast side of Tenaya Canyon. During the ice ages, that crest of rock helped guide one of two major glaciers toward Yosemite Valley. The ice that ground along the flanks of Clouds Rest reached depths of 2,000 feet and coalesced along the base of Half Dome with another glacier of equal magnitude that flowed in from the right. The combined glaciers filled the main Yosemite Valley and gathered even more ice from tributary glaciers that entered laterally from hanging valleys such as the one that launches Bridalveil Fall.

■ **Half Dome** ■ Perhaps the best-known landmark in Yosemite, Half Dome stands nearly 5,000 feet above the floor of Yosemite Valley. The glaciers that coalesced along the base of Half Dome never overrode its crest. Half Dome, like El Capitan, is a "nunatak," that is, a mountain peak that projected above the deepest glacial ice. Its distinctive shape—rounded on one side, flat on the other—was determined mainly by the types of joints within the rock. Joints along its north face are vertical, while those along its crest are concentric.

■ **Cathedral Rocks** ■ Widely separated vertical joints guided the erosion and weathering process that shaped this set of three massive buttresses. Echoing one another's form in an ascending series, the three summits stand at elevations of roughly 5,600, 6,500, and 6,850 feet.

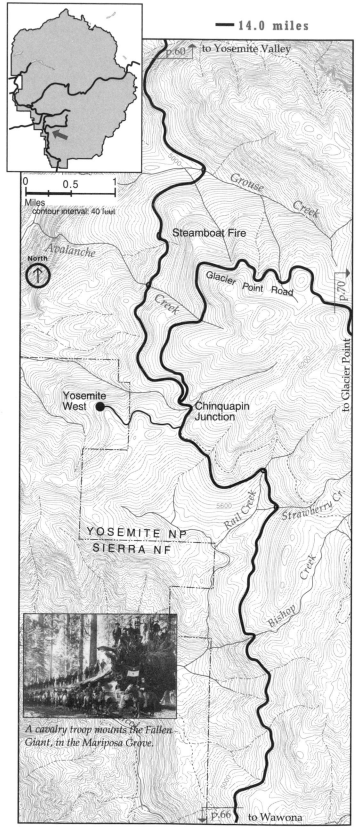

— 14.0 miles

p.60 ↑ to Yosemite Valley

Grouse Creek

Steamboat Fire

Glacier Point Road

p.70 →

Avalanche

North

Miles
contour interval: 40 feet

0   0.5   1

Creek

to Glacier Point

Yosemite West

Chinquapin Junction

Rail Creek

Strawberry Cr.

5600

YOSEMITE NP
SIERRA NF

Bishop Creek

A cavalry troop mounts the Fallen Giant, in the Mariposa Grove.

↓ p.66 to Wawona

Grouse Creek: Worth a quick stop to check out wet habitat wildflowers, Grouse Creek is a dependable late-summer home for the park's namesake flower, the Yosemite aster. This variation of *Aster occidentalis* was first collected and described for science in 1877 by Joseph Hooker and Asa Gray during a jaunt near Vernal Fall.

Steamboat Fire: This signed turnout on the west side of the road lies at the margin of the 1990 Steamboat Fire, a lightning-caused blaze that forced the evacuation of West Yosemite and left a patchwork of scorched terrain over an area of 8,000 acres. In the burned area, silvered snags protrude from a plush understory of shrubs and ponderosa pine saplings, some of which have already reached 15 feet in height. A stand of untouched incense cedars and ponderosa pines shade the turnout. An outcrop of rock farther down the slope overlooks the Merced River Canyon.

Avalanche Creek: A moist recess in the mixed conifer forest, Avalanche Creek's drainage supports Solomon's seal, trail plant, giant trillium, and California bluebell. Denizens of the surrounding forest include two types of owls—the great horned owl and its diminutive cousin, the northern pygmy owl. Standing just seven inches tall, the pygmy owl regularly attacks rodents that outweigh it. Desperate skirmishes ensue, and the owl often is dragged some distance by its meal before it can settle in for the feast.

Chinquapin Junction: Named for a conspicuous broadleaf evergreen shrub, this junction is the start of the Glacier Point Road *(see pp. 70–79)*, which bowls along for 16 miles to a drop away vista of Yosemite Valley and the mountains to the east.

Rail and Strawberry Creeks: Flowing within a half-mile of one another, these two small, shaded creeks provide habitat for a variety of wildflowers. At Rail Creek, look for common monkey flowers, lupine, self-heal, and narrowleaf lotus. Strawberry Creek harbors wild strawberry, Indian rhubarb, small leopard lily, and pinedrops. Self-heal was used traditionally in teas and poultices as a remedy for all manner of ills, including sore throats, mouth sores, fevers, nausea, ulcers, and insect bites.

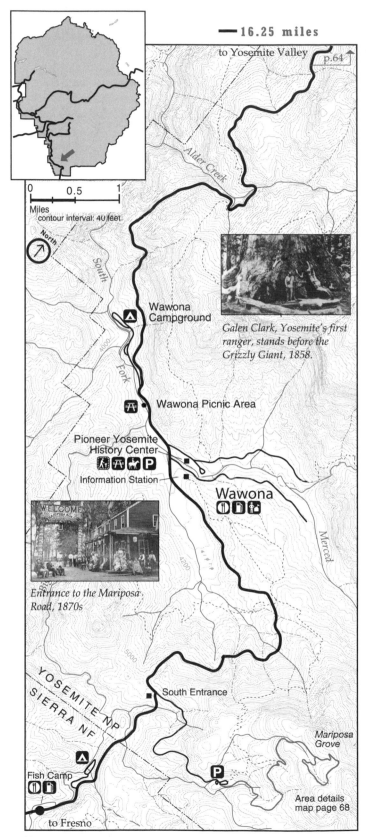

to Yosemite Valley p.64

Alder Creek

0   0.5   1
Miles
contour interval: 40 feet

North

South

4000

Wawona
Campground

Galen Clark, Yosemite's first ranger, stands before the Grizzly Giant, 1858.

Fork

Wawona Picnic Area

Pioneer Yosemite
History Center

Information Station

Wawona

WELCOME

Entrance to the Mariposa Road, 1870s

4200

Merced

5000

YOSEMITE NP

SIERRA NF

South Entrance

Mariposa Grove

Fish Camp

P

Area details
map page 68

to Fresno

Alder Creek: From Alder Creek, the highway descends about 1,000 feet and drops away from the mixed conifer forest into the oak woodland forest belt. Here, at an elevation of about 4,000 feet, California black oak and canyon live oak become far more common and ponderosa pine and incense cedar remain as the predominant conifers.

Wawona Campground: From 1891 to 1906, this site served as the principal encampment for soldiers administering Yosemite. It was named Camp A.E. Wood, after the first military superintendent of the park.

Wawona Picnic Area: Shaded by large incense cedars and ponderosa pines, this lovely picnic area along the South Fork Merced River beckons with an exceptional swimming hole. A comfortable wading depth, the crystalline river washes over a bed of rounded stones the size of melons. Here and there the river slides past a tilted granite slab, carves out a deeper, emerald green pool, and lines the bottom with fine white sand. Among the cracks in the rocks, you might spot a young Gilbert's skink, a small lizard-like creature with long black and white stripes and a bright blue tail that breaks off when attacked by a predator.

Pioneer Yosemite History Center: Located along the banks of the South Fork Merced River, the history center is a collection of historic, pioneer-era buildings that have been moved to the site and now provide a forum for living history reenactors, including the only stagecoach driver/ranger in the National Park Service. Cross the river on the 1875 covered bridge and amble among the structures, each of which represents a different era in Yosemite's history. Buildings include an operating blacksmithy, homestead cabin, ranger patrol cabin, bakery, and a Wells Fargo office where you can book a stagecoach ride for a few dollars.

Wawona: This small community began in 1857 as a rustic stage stop run by Galen Clark for visitors traveling between the Mariposa Grove and Yosemite Valley. In the 1870s, Clark sold out to the Washburn family, which opened the gracious Wawona Hotel in 1879. The large, Victorian-style hostelry opens its lobby, porches, restaurants, bars, and golf course to the general public.

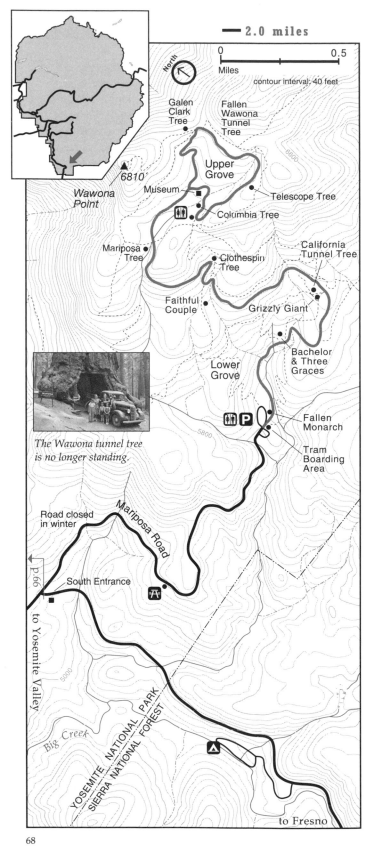

2.0 miles

0   0.5
Miles
contour interval: 40 feet

North

Galen
Clark
Tree

Fallen
Wawona
Tunnel
Tree

6810'

Wawona
Point

Upper
Grove

Museum

Telescope Tree

Columbia Tree

Mariposa
Tree

Clothespin
Tree

California
Tunnel Tree

Faithful
Couple

Grizzly Giant

Bachelor
& Three
Graces

Lower
Grove

Fallen
Monarch

Tram
Boarding
Area

*The Wawona tunnel tree
is no longer standing.*

Road closed
in winter

Mariposa Road

p.66

South Entrance

to Yosemite Valley

Big Creek

YOSEMITE NATIONAL PARK

SIERRA NATIONAL FOREST

to Fresno

68

Mariposa Grove: Largest of Yosemite's three sequoia groves, this 250-acre area contains approximately 500 colossal sequoias, including some of the finest specimens of the big tree found anywhere in the world. To thoroughly explore the grove's upper and lower sections and the Mariposa Grove Museum use the generous network of trails or the open-air tram. Discover the spectacular overlook of the valley at Wawona Point.

The giant sequoia is the world's largest non-clonal living thing. In terms of volume, a single sequoia may contain as much wood as is found on one acre of prime Pacific Northwest forest. It is also one of the fastest growing and oldest trees in the world, adding as much to its bulk each year as the volume of a tree 150 feet tall and 18 inches in diameter. Typically the trees attain heights of 150 to 250 feet and reach trunk diameters of 10 to 25 feet. Their thick, plate-like bark contains high concentrations of tannic acid and resists both fire and insects. Giant sequoias can live for more than 3,000 years and do not die from old age; instead, they generally succumb to toppling. Despite its resistance to disease, insects, and fire, the sequoia is a relatively rare tree in the wild, confined to about 75 groves along the western slope of the Sierra Nevada at 5,000 to 7,000 feet of elevation.

Columbia Tree is the tallest tree in the grove, about 290 feet high. Beyond it stands the Mariposa Grove Museum, a cabin built in 1864 by Galen Clark at the feet of a pair of colossal sequoias.

Fire burned away much of the inside of the **Clothespin Tree**, yet it remains healthy and continues to produce cones. For seed dispersal, sequoias depend in part upon Douglas' squirrels, which eat the fleshy green scales of the cone and scatter the seeds. A single squirrel can cut away more than 500 cones in just a half hour; one busy squirrel observed in 1905 cut 12,000 cones in a single day.

The **Grizzly Giant,** oldest sequoia in the grove, is thought to have thrived for approximately 1,800 years. About 200 feet tall, the tree has a trunk diameter of more than 30 feet.

The **Fallen Monarch** fell several hundred years ago and broke into pieces. Its shallow root system demonstrates why sequoias are susceptible to toppling, and the mass of wood that survives demonstrates the heartwood's resistance to decay.

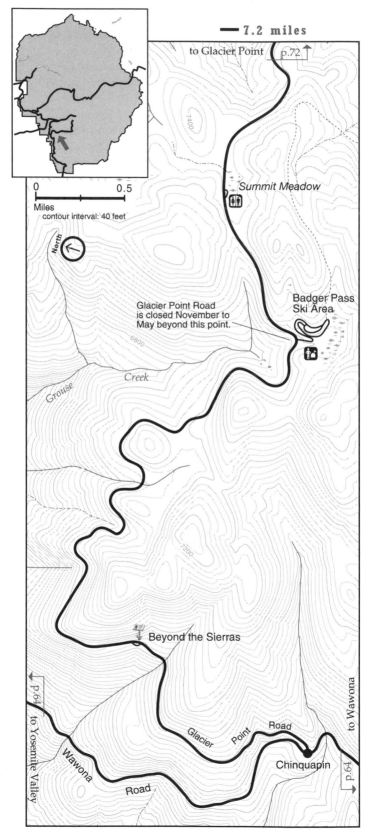

7.2 miles

to Glacier Point p.72

Summit Meadow

Badger Pass
Ski Area

Glacier Point Road
is closed November to
May beyond this point.

Grouse   Creek

North

0   0.5

Miles
contour interval: 40 feet

6800

7200

Beyond the Sierras

p.64

to Yosemite Valley

Wawona
Road

Glacier   Point   Road

Chinquapin

to Wawona

p.64

Glacier Point Road

Summit Meadow: In their haste to reach Glacier Point, most visitors rush past this small opening in the lodgepole pine/red fir forest. Moist, spongy, dotted with small ponds, Summit Meadow rarely dries out completely, which extends the peak of its wildflower season. Look for bistort, shooting star, camas lilies, and Sierra rein orchids. Later, look for cow parsnip, corn lilies, and a vivid yellow blossom on a tall, slender stem that bears a curious name: Bigelow's sneezeweed.

Nature Note ■ Sugar Pine: The tallest and largest of the world's 100 species of pine trees, sugar pines also bear the world's longest cone. Old-growth specimens commonly reach 200 feet in height with trunk diameters of 6 to 7 feet. Large trees produce about 100 cones each year. Most of the cones measure between 11 and 18 inches, with a record one 28 inches. Douglas' squirrels, or chickarees, scramble through the branches, cutting away the cones that weigh up to four pounds and that hit the ground with surprising force. The squirrels, weighing in at less than a pound, then shred the cones for nuts the size of corn kernels. The sugar pine gets its name from the syrupy resin it exudes when wounded; the crystallized resin was prized as a delicacy among Native Americans. ■

Beyond the Sierra: An opening in the trees affords a panoramic vista of terraced mountain crests stepping off to the hazy west. On clear days one can see the eastern rim of the San Joaquin Valley and even the distant crest of the Coast Ranges, but air pollution can often obscure the view. While sugar pines tower overhead, look for western fence lizards scurrying underfoot.

Chinquapin Junction: Located at the intersection of the Glacier Point and Wawona Roads, Chinquapin Junction takes its name from a broad-leafed evergreen shrub that grows in warm, open sites over a broad elevation range (3,000 to 8,000 feet). About four feet high and related to the chestnut, it bears a prickly, burr-like fruit about three inches in diameter that contains a nut similar in flavor to the hazelnut. Not far from the junction's rest area (about 300 yards toward Yosemite Valley), look for seep springs that support a vibrant display of mosses, ferns, and wildflowers that include scarlet monkey flower, narrowleaf lotus, and orchids.

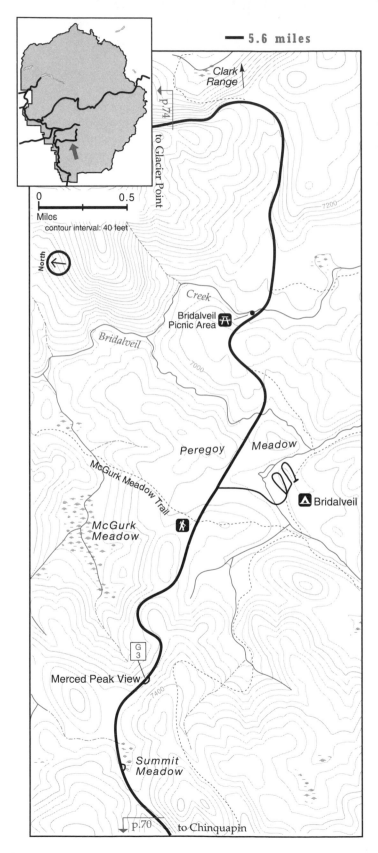

5.6 miles

Clark Range

p.74

to Glacier Point

0   0.5
Miles
contour interval: 40 feet

North

7200

Creek

Bridalveil
Picnic Area

Bridalveil

7000

Peregoy   Meadow

McGurk Meadow Trail

Bridalveil

McGurk
Meadow

G
3
Merced Peak View

7400

Summit
Meadow

p.70
to Chinquapin

Clark Range View: As the highway bends north, fabulous views of the Clark Range open up to the east. A turnout at the north end of this precipitous stretch of road offers a chance to double back on foot for an unobstructed view. The Clark Range is named for Galen Clark, appointed the first guardian of the park after Yosemite Valley and the Mariposa Big Tree Grove were granted in 1864 to California as a public trust. The range includes Mount Clark, elevation 11,522 feet, Merced Peak and, between them, aptly named Red Peak.

Bridalveil Creek Picnic Area: Here, sun-dappled Bridalveil Creek splashes among large gray boulders and slabs of granite, its banks cushioned by verdant plants and colorful blossoms that draw in butterflies.

Peregoy Meadow: A relatively dry meadow that spans both sides of the highway, Peregoy Meadow was named after Charles Peregoy, who ran a rustic hotel nearby called the Mountain View House, which thrived from 1869 to 1875. Larkspur, a deep purple flower, now prospers here, as do many types of small rodents, including mice, shrews, and voles.

McGurk Meadow Trail: This 15- to 20-minute stroll (2.0-mile round trip; 300-foot elevation gain) through lodgepole pine forest leads to a boardwalk bridge over a small stream and offers a lovely view of breezy McGurk Meadow. The water that slowly filters through this meadow eventually joins tributary streams and leaps from the brink of Bridalveil Fall in Yosemite Valley. Look for lupine and purple asters along the trail, deer in the meadow, and Douglas' squirrels and chickadees among the trees.

Merced Peak: As the highway descends from Summit Meadow, Merced Peak, elevation 11,726 feet, stands dead ahead, framed at this point by roadside trees. The headwaters of the Merced River gather along the flanks of the peak.

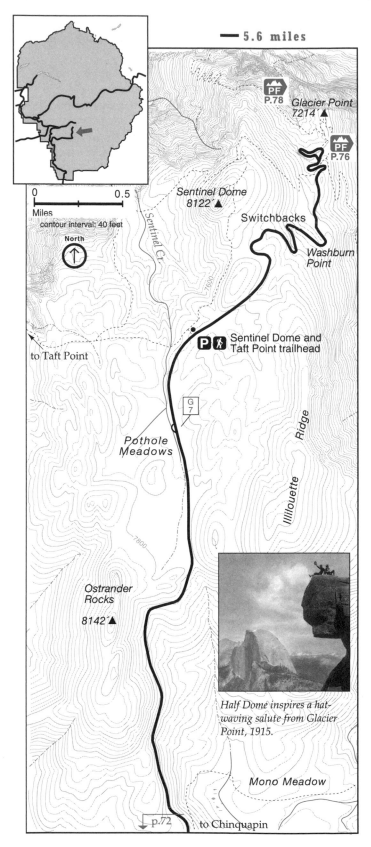

PF
P.78

Glacier Point
7214′ ▲

PF
P.76

Sentinel Dome
8122′ ▲

Switchbacks

*Washburn
Point*

0   0.5
Miles
contour interval: 40 feet

North
↑

Sentinel Cr.

7500

← to Taft Point

P 🚶 Sentinel Dome and
Taft Point trailhead

G
7

*Pothole
Meadows*

Illilouette Ridge

7800

*Ostrander
Rocks*

8142′ ▲

*Half Dome inspires a hat-
waving salute from Glacier
Point, 1915.*

Mono Meadow

↓
p.72
to Chinquapin

74

Glacier Point: Poised 3,200 feet above Yosemite Valley, Glacier Point provides two jaw-dropping vistas: first, a comprehensive prospect of the domes, glacial troughs, and rambling country of the High Sierra; second, a view down Yosemite Valley as far as Yosemite Falls. Always crowded, especially at sunset, Glacier Point is laced by short, meandering paths and picketed with interpretive signs and peaks finders. At night it offers an unparalleled vantage point for stargazing.

While at Glacier Point, consider hiking down to Illilouette Fall (4.6-mile round trip; 1,300-foot elevation change), or arrange for a shuttle and hike all the way down to Happy Isles via Nevada and Vernal Falls (9.1 miles; 3,200-foot elevation drop). Shuttle transportation for hikers books up quickly, so be sure to plan ahead and make a reservation early.

Washburn Point: Shaded by towering red firs, this ledge offers a sweeping vista of the High Sierra and the best overall view of Vernal and Nevada Falls in the park. This pair of falls along the Merced River spills over the Giant's Staircase, a glaciated flight of granite steps that rises to Little Yosemite Valley. The upper fall, Nevada, plunges 594 feet; Vernal, 317 feet.

Sentinel Dome and Taft Point: Nothing short of exhilarating, this wonderful loop trail (4.0-mile round trip; 600-foot elevation gain) links two of the most spectacular vantage points in the park with a walk along the very rim of Yosemite Valley. The route begins to the left, with a gradual descent though open forest to Taft Point, a granite promontory that projects 3,500 feet above the valley floor (not a good place for small children). The panoramic view takes in El Capitan, the Three Brothers, Yosemite Falls, and the meandering Merced River. Western fence lizards dart among the cracks. White-throated swifts—that may fly as many as a million miles during a normal lifespan—tumble and dive in the void.

The route doubles back about half-way to the parking lot, then branches to the left and bounds along through the forest, occasionally nipping out to the very edge of the cliffs. The trail remains in shade and climbs gradually to the north side of Sentinel Dome and its 8,122-foot summit. Here an intoxicating 360-degree vista awaits. A peaks finder embedded in a large glacial erratic identifies prominent landmarks.

Half Dome from Glacier Point Amphitheater

Mount Hoffman
10,852 feet

Mount Watkins
8,500 feet

Clouds Rest
9,926 feet

Vogelsang Peak
11,516 feet

Mount Clark
11,522 feet

Basket Dome
7,612 feet

Tenaya Peak
10,301 feet

Echo Peaks

Half Dome
8,842 feet

Liberty Cap
7,076 feet

Nevada
Fall

Tenaya Canyon

Reading the Landscape

■ **Half Dome** ■ The central, dominant landmark visible from Glacier Point, Half Dome may look a bit like a split sphere but it is not. In fact, it is a relatively narrow protrusion of dense granodiorite that has taken on its distinctive shape due to the orientation of joints within the rock.

Its steep, northwest face formed along parallel vertical joints: thin slabs of rock were loosened by weathering and fell away, layer by layer. During the Pleistocene epoch, the great Tenaya Glacier slid along Half Dome's steep face, plucking away more slabs and clearing away the accumulated talus.

The rounded slopes of Half Dome also owe their shape to joints within the rock, but these are concentric, like those that separate the layers of an onion. As with the park's other exfoliation domes, these joints formed as the great weight of overlying rocks eroded away. The upper surface of the granitic batholith expanded slightly and the joints formed parallel with its outer surface.

■ **Liberty Cap and Mount Broderick** ■ Both of these prominent domes were completely overridden by glaciers during the height of the ice ages. While the Tenaya Glacier slid past Half Dome's northwest face, another colossal glacier moved down the Little Yosemite Valley and buried Liberty Cap and Mount Broderick in hundreds of feet of moving ice. The two glaciers coalesced below Half Dome and continued down the main Yosemite Valley, filling it nearly to its brim. Both Liberty Cap and Mount Broderick bear the characteristics of a roche moutonnee: a smooth, rounded, and polished side where the ice approached and overrode the domes; and a steep side where the ice flowed away from the domes, plucking away slabs of rock as it passed.

■ **Nevada Fall** ■ This grand plume of Merced River white water plunges 594 feet and is the higher of two major waterfalls that stairstep into Yosemite Valley from the Little Yosemite Valley. The other, Vernal Fall, is masked by forest at this point and cannot be seen. Both falls descend giant glacial steps that formed as the ice moved down the valley, plucking out blocks of closely jointed bedrock from between bands of massive granite. The resulting gorge, known sometimes as the Giant's Staircase, is one of the most heavily traveled day-hike routes in Yosemite.

Yosemite Valley from Glacier Point

Yosemite Falls

Yosemite Village

Royal Arches

North Dome 7,525 feet

Basket Dome 7,612 feet

Mirror Lake 12,324 feet

Clouds Rest 9,926 feet

Half Dome 8,842 feet

TENAYA CANYON

YOSEMITE VALLEY

Reading the Landscape

■ **Yosemite's Glaciers** ■ The details of Yosemite's glacial history remain obscure and hotly contested by geologists, but most agree that the park experienced four major periods of glaciation, each with many advances and retreats. Although the advances and retreats varied in terms of duration and depth of ice, the landscape visible from this point today clearly shows the major routes of glacial travel. Broadly speaking, glaciers moving down from Tenaya Canyon and Little Yosemite Valley coalesced under Half Dome and proceeded down the main Yosemite Valley.

The oldest and most extensive glaciation predates the last major advance of continental glaciers in North America. It spread far and wide across the uplands to the east and inundated virtually all of the landmarks one sees from here, with the exception of Half Dome. The second major glaciation reached its maximum about 70,000 years ago and also formed major, valley-filling glaciers. The two most recent advances formed glaciers that traveled down the previous routes as far as Bridalveil Fall, but the ice was neither as thick nor as erosive as glaciers of the previous ice ages. The most recent glaciation peaked about 20,000 years ago and ended about 10,000 years ago.

■ **Royal Arches** ■ A classic example of how exfoliation can produce arches on the steep sides of domes, this formation is a series of recessed arches set back into a main arch, which soars a thousand feet above the valley floor. Geologists think that the Tenaya Glacier probably gouged away the lower parts of the concentric shells of rock and undermined them.

■ **Yosemite Lake** ■ During glacial advances and retreats, a short-lived lake sometimes formed on the floor of Yosemite Valley. When the most recent glacial advance ended, a shallow lake roughly 5.5 miles long formed behind a recessional moraine. The lake soon filled in with sediment and disappeared, leaving swampy meadows.

■ **Yosemite Falls** ■ This vantage point is one of the few in the park that offers a comprehensive view of all three sections of Yosemite Falls: the Upper Fall, 1,430 feet; the Middle Cascade, 675 feet; and the Lower Fall, 320 feet.

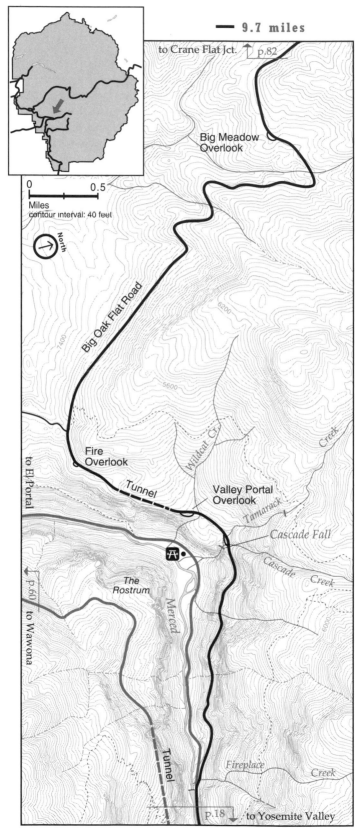

to Crane Flat Jct. ↑ p.82

Big Meadow Overlook

0   0.5
Miles
contour interval: 40 feet

North

Big Oak Flat Road

7400

6200

5600

Wildcat Cr.

Creek

Fire Overlook

Tunnel

Valley Portal Overlook

Tamarack

Cascade Fall

to El Portal

The Rostrum

Merced

Cascade Creek

6000

p.60

to Wawona

Tunnel

Fireplace Creek

p.18 ↓ to Yosemite Valley

Big Oak Flat Drive

Fire Overlook: This signed turnout offers southbound travelers their first glimpse of Yosemite Valley landmarks. From here, the vertical faces of El Capitan (left) and Half Dome (right) seem nearly to touch one another, even though they stand about six miles apart. Best seen in afternoon or evening light, the view draws many admirers. It is possible to leave behind the clamber of the parking area by scrambling down the rocks a short distance.

The turnout also overlooks a widespread patchwork of burned terrain—the result of major wildfires that ignited during the dry summer of 1990 and scorched 24,000 acres in two weeks. Fire destroys, it also creates new opportunities for plants and animals. It admits sunlight onto the forest floor, encouraging the growth of deciduous shrubs and other plants that provide food for black bears, mule deer, and a host of smaller animals.

Tunnel: The first and longest of three tunnels on the north side of the valley, this 0.4-mile tunnel avoids a sheer rock face that plunges 1,200 feet to the Merced River.

Valley Portal Overlook: Although it lacks vistas of El Capitan and Half Dome, this vantage point overlooks the Merced River Gorge and provides a view that takes in Bridalveil Fall and the rim of its hanging valley, Cathedral Rocks, and Sentinel Dome. The river, 1,100 feet below, rushes straight toward the overlook, then makes a sharp bend to the south, following the course of glaciers that filled Yosemite Valley with varying levels of ice during at least four major ice ages. At least one early glaciation filled the valley to its very rim, completely overriding Cathedral Rocks and the Valley Portal Overlook. The latest glaciation reached its maximum extent about 20,000 years ago, advancing only to the vicinity of Cathedral Rocks, and reaching just partway up the valley's cliff walls.

Cascade Fall: Two stone bridges in quick succession span Tamarack and Cascade creeks, which splash over steep jumbles of rock above the road, then join below and leap from the cliffs to form 500-foot Cascade Fall. Informal trails lead below the road to views of the falls, but they can be extremely dangerous, especially in high-water months.

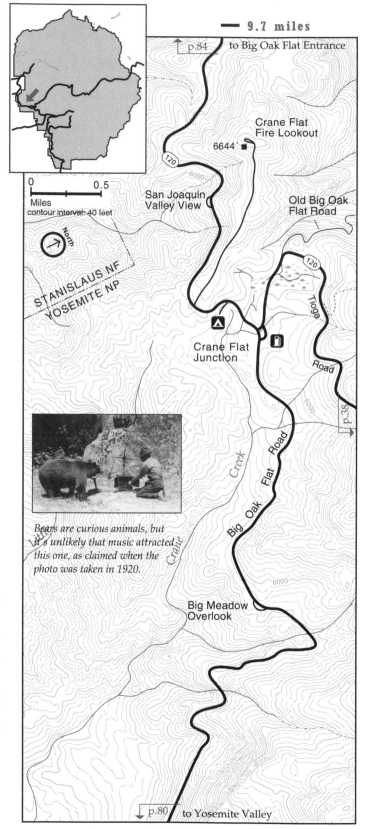

to Big Oak Flat Entrance ← p.84

— 9.7 miles

Crane Flat
Fire Lookout

6644

San Joaquin
Valley View

Old Big Oak
Flat Road

120

Tioga Road

STANISLAUS NF
YOSEMITE NP

0   0.5
Miles
contour interval: 40 feet

North

Crane Flat
Junction

p.38 →

Crane Creek

Big Oak Flat Road

*Bears are curious animals, but
it's unlikely that music attracted
this one, as claimed when the
photo was taken in 1920.*

Big Meadow
Overlook

to Yosemite Valley ← p.80

Crane Flat Fire Lookout: Perched atop an open ridge at approximately 6,600 feet, this fire lookout offers a comprehensive vista of Yosemite's high country, including peaks in the Clark Range and Half Dome. The route (3.2-mile round trip) climbs about 500 feet through a mixed conifer forest of ponderosa pine, sugar pine, white fir, incense cedar, and Douglas fir. Along the way, look for Douglas' squirrels; nattering, territorial, and busy, these small squirrels eat conifer shoots and other green plants, nuts, berries, and mushrooms.

Crane Flat Junction: From this intersection, the Tioga Road *(see pp. 38–59)* climbs eastward to the crest of the Sierras at Tioga Pass and leads to some of the park's best-known landmarks outside Yosemite Valley: Olmsted Point, Tenaya Lake, and Tuolumne Meadows. The trailhead for the Tuolumne Grove of giant sequoias lies just a short distance up the road.

In the forests around Crane Flat live mule deer, mountain lions, black bears, coyotes, bobcats, bushy-tailed wood rats, porcupines, weasels, and northern flying squirrels. Quite common but rarely seen because it is active at night, the northern flying squirrel glides from tree to tree by spreading its legs and stretching its flight skin, which acts like a sail.

Also common but rarely seen, the porcupine is best known for the 30,000 quills that protectively adorn its body. Though it cannot throw its quills, the porcupine can embed them in a predator with a quick flash of its tail. A good climber, the porcupine uses the quills on the underside of its tail to keep it from sliding back down the tree trunk.

Big Meadow Overlook: This turnout overlooks Big Meadow, a large opening in the forest about 1,400 feet below the highway. A former lake bed, Big Meadow filled in with soil that washed down from surrounding slopes. Trees gradually invaded the meadow and, if they had been left unchecked, they might have absorbed the meadow into the forest. However, a 1990 wildfire not only checked the progress of the forest into Big Meadow but also destroyed most of the adjacent community of Foresta.

Trees at this turnout include some very large examples of incense cedar, which protects itself from ground fires with a basal bark up to six inches thick.

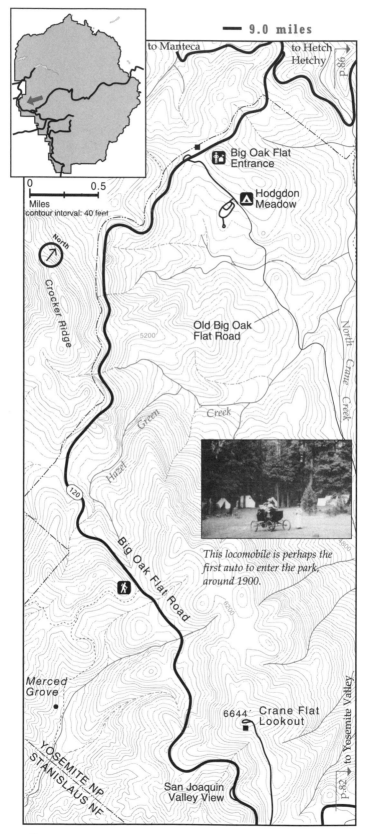

to Manteca

to Hetch
Hetchy

p. 86

Big Oak Flat
Entrance

Hodgdon
Meadow

Crocker Ridge

North

Old Big Oak
Flat Road

North Crane Creek

Green Creek

Hazel Creek

120

This locomobile is perhaps the first auto to enter the park, around 1900.

Big Oak Flat Road

6200

4800

Merced
Grove

YOSEMITE NP
STANISLAUS NF

6644
Crane Flat
Lookout

San Joaquin
Valley View

to Yosemite Valley

p. 82

Miles
contour interval: 40 feet

0   0.5

5200

Big Oak Flat Entrance Station: The park's northwest entrance is a major access point for visitors coming from San Francisco. On busy weekends, traffic can back up for as far as three to four miles.

Hodgdon Meadow: A serpentine opening in the mixed conifer forest, Hodgdon Meadow lies along the Old Big Oak Flat Road, just beyond today's group campsites in the Hodgdon Meadow Campground. The meadow attracts mule deer and occasional black bears, and it is a likely hunting ground for great horned owls. This large owl stands 18 to 25 inches tall, has a wingspan up to 60 inches, and hunts in low light conditions when its prey is most active. The great horned owl feeds on small shrews, ground squirrels, amphibians, rabbits, and other birds—even hawks.

Old Big Oak Flat Road: Part of the original route into Yosemite Valley, this old road is closed now to all but foot and bike traffic. It connects Hodgdon Meadow with the Tuolumne Grove (4.1 miles one way; 1,000-foot elevation gain) and with the Tioga Road at Crane Flat (another 2 miles with an additional elevation gain of 500 feet). The route climbs gradually through the mixed conifer forest of ponderosa pine, incense cedar, Douglas fir, Jeffrey pine, sugar pine, and white fir.

Merced Grove: Smallest of the park's three giant sequoia groves and often overlooked, the Merced Grove contains about a dozen mammoth sequoias and many saplings. Because it is lightly visited, this grove may offer the most rewarding sequoia experience in the park: silence, seclusion, unobscured access to the very bases of the trees. The trail (3.0-mile round trip; 500-foot elevation gain) descends steadily through a forest of large white firs, Douglas firs, and sugar pines to a row of a half dozen sequoias, which rise more than 200 feet from a shrubby understory that includes mountain dogwood. Larger examples of the massive, cinnamon-brown trunks can be found a short distance down the trail near a park service cabin.

San Joaquin Valley View: This stop provides an excellent vista of a procession of rugged, forested ridge tops stepping away to the west as far as the San Joaquin Valley. On rare days when air pollution does not obscure the view, one can even see the Coast Range.

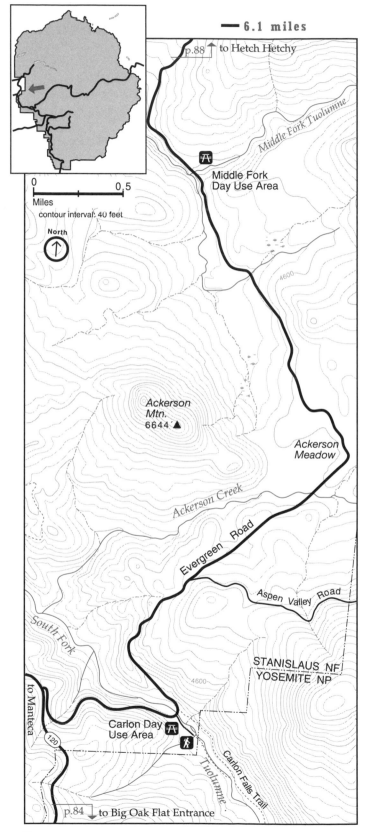

p.88 ↑ to Hetch Hetchy

Middle Fork Tuolumne

Middle Fork
Day Use Area

4600

Ackerson
Mtn.
6644 ▲

Ackerson
Meadow

Ackerson Creek

Evergreen Road

Aspen Valley Road

South Fork

STANISLAUS NF
YOSEMITE NP

4600

to Manteca

120

Carlon Day
Use Area

Tuolumne

Carlon Falls Trail

p.84 ↓ to Big Oak Flat Entrance

0   0.5
Miles
contour interval: 40 feet

North
↑

Hetch Hetchy Road

Middle Fork Day Use Area: Breezy, cool, and peaceful, this picnic area overlooks a narrow, rock-lined canyon of the Middle Fork Tuolumne River. Across the road, trails zigzag down to enticing swimming holes. Mountain lions, rarely seen, hunt for mule deer and other animals in mountainous, semiarid terrain such as that traversed by Evergreen Road. Solitary ambush hunters, mountain lions stalk to within 30 feet of their prey, then rush forward, leap on the victim's back, and kill with a bite to the neck. Besides deer, mountain lions feed on coyotes, porcupines, mice, hares, raccoons, and even grasshoppers.

Ackerson Meadow: Homesteaded in the 19th century, this expansive grass meadow is still in private hands. From the road, however, one can spot mule deer early and late in the day. The meadow supports a host of small rodents that attract coyotes, foxes, and winged predators including red-tailed hawks and various owls. Except for red-taileds and kestrels, which are largely summer residents, raptors are rare in the park. Three types of owls, however, are fairly common: the great horned, northern pygmy, and flammulated.

Carlon Day Use Area: Nestled along the banks of the South Fork Tuolumne River, this picnic area takes its name from Dan and Donna Carlon, owners of the Carl Inn, an early resort that operated from 1916 to 1930 in a meadow just a quarter mile above the bridge. Look for belted kingfishers perched on bare branches beside the stream. A smallish bird with an outsized head and bill, the kingfisher dives headfirst into the water to catch fish up to two feet beneath the surface.

Carlon Falls Trail: From the picnic area, the trail (4.0-mile round trip; negligible elevation gain) ambles along the river through a deep and at times soggy forest of old-growth pine, fir, oak, and incense cedar to a stair-stepping cascade that drops a total of 50 feet in three separate leaps. Broad, gently sloping slabs of granite studded with boulders line the banks of the river at the falls and form deep pools that draw many swimmers and sunbathers. In exposed granite surfaces, look for potholes that are enlarged every spring by trapped sand, gravel, and stones that swirl around the interiors of the potholes and act as drill bits.

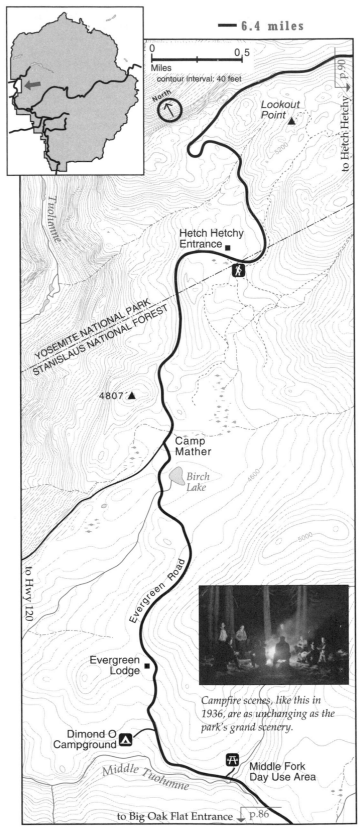

0   0.5

Miles
contour interval: 40 feet

North

Lookout Point ▲

to Hetch Hetchy → p.90

Hetch Hetchy
Entrance ■

Tuolumne

YOSEMITE NATIONAL PARK
STANISLAUS NATIONAL FOREST

4807 ▲

Camp
Mather

*Birch
Lake*

to Hwy 120

Evergreen Road

Evergreen
Lodge ■

*Campfire scenes, like this in
1936, are as unchanging as the
park's grand scenery.*

Dimond O
Campground ▲

Middle Tuolumne

Middle Fork
Day Use Area

to Big Oak Flat Entrance ↓ p.86

Hetch Hetchy Entrance Station: Sleepiest of Yosemite's four entrance stations, the Hetch Hetchy stands in the shade of incense cedars and ponderosa pines. Just beyond it and on the right is a trailhead for Lookout Point, a bald knob of granite that provides a distant view of O'Shaughnessy Dam and the Hetch Hetchy Reservoir (2.6-mile round trip; 300-foot elevation gain). At its best in the spring, the hike climbs from forest through sparse foothills vegetation. This is good country for spotting rattlesnakes, alligator lizards, and mountain quail.

Camp Mather: Named for Stephen Mather, first director of the National Park Service, this private summer camp is operated by the City of San Francisco for its employees and their families. The road passes through Camp Mather and, turning right, picks up the same route followed by the Hetch Hetchy Railroad during construction of the O'Shaughnessy Dam. Between 1914 and 1923 the railroad carried men, materials, and machinery to the dam's construction site.

Evergreen Lodge: Established during the 1920s, Evergreen Lodge offers rustic accommodations and a good restaurant that draw big crowds in the summer months. Guests here and at Camp Mather (just down the road) largely account for the number of bicyclists on this narrow road.

Nature Note ▪ Foothills Life Zone: As the road descends toward Hetch Hetchy Reservoir, it dips into the Foothills Life Zone, a hotter, drier zone that extends west of the park down to elevations of 500 feet. Here plants include gray pine, blue oak, interior live oak, scrub oak, chamise, toyon, and other chaparral plants. Mammals include the dusky-footed wood rat, spotted skunk, and bobcat. In the immediate vicinity, mountain quail are commonly seen during spring and early summer. About the size of a small pigeon, this gray-and-rust colored brown bird sports a pair of rakish feathers that sweep back from the top of its head. Although it flies when threatened, this quail prefers to walk. After nesting, small family groups travel many miles on foot as they move to lower elevations. ▪

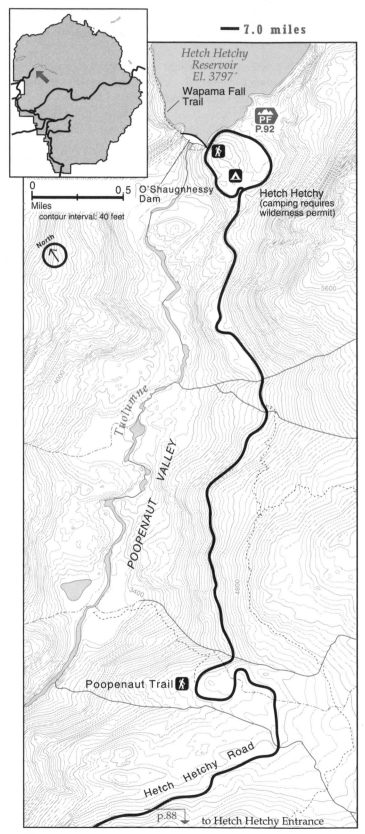

7.0 miles

Hetch Hetchy Reservoir El. 3797´

Wapama Fall Trail

PF P.92

O'Shaugnhessy Dam

Hetch Hetchy (camping requires wilderness permit)

0   0.5
Miles
contour interval: 40 feet

North

5600

Tuolumne

POOPENAUT VALLEY

4000

3400

4800

Poopenaut Trail

Hetch Hetchy Road

p.88 → to Hetch Hetchy Entrance

Wapama Fall Trail: This easy, nearly level trail hugs the north shore of Hetch Hetchy Reservoir and leads to two major waterfalls that spill from the sheer granite walls. The first, Tueeulala, plunges roughly 1,000 feet; Wapama, about 1,400 feet. In May, great numbers of California newts migrate across the trail as they make their way back to their birthplace streams to breed.

O'Shaughnessy Dam: Built between 1914 and 1923 and then expanded during the late 1930s, O'Shaughnessy Dam impounds the Tuolumne River to supply San Francisco with power and drinking water. The wall of concrete rises 317 feet, and its rim spans the valley for a distance of 600 feet. The prospect of such a structure in any national park, but especially Yosemite, horrified John Muir. "Dam Hetch Hetchy!" he wrote. "As well dam for water-tanks the people's cathedrals and churches, for no holier temple has ever been consecrated by the heart of man." He led a long fight against the dam, characterizing its supporters as "these temple destroyers, devotees of ravaging commercialism, seem to have a perfect contempt for Nature, and, instead of lifting their eyes to the God of the mountains, lift them to the Almighty Dollar."

Muir died the year construction began.

Hetch Hetchy Reservoir: Eight miles long and up to 360 feet deep, this reservoir of the Tuolumne River submerges much of a glacially carved valley that once rivaled Yosemite for beauty.

"I have always called it the 'Tuolumne Yosemite,'" wrote John Muir, "for it is a wonderfully exact counterpart of the Merced Yosemite, not only in its sublime rocks and waterfalls but in the gardens, groves and meadows of its flowery park-like floor."

Poopenaut Trail: Short but steep, this 2.0-mile round-trip hike drops 1,250 vertical feet into the Poopenaut Valley and offers solitude, a pleasant place to swim or fish along the Tuolumne River, and a strenuous climb back to the road. The valley lies within the Foothills Life Zone, and is therefore rich in amphibians and reptiles, including salamanders, toads, frogs, lizards, and snakes. One of the foothills snakes, the racer, can move as fast as a person can run and might just be the fastest of all snakes.

Hetch Hetchy Reservoir

Tueeulala Falls

Wapama Falls

Hetch Hetchy Dome
6,165 feet

Kolana Rock
5,772 feet

HETCH HETCHY RESERVOIR (3,797 feet)

Hetch Hetchy Valley
Floor (approx. 3,500 feet)

Reading the Landscape

■ **Tueeulala Falls** ■ John Muir, an aficionado of waterfalls, called this 1,000-foot, free-falling plume "the most graceful fall I have ever seen." Muir compared Tueeulala's "silvery scarf" to Bridalveil Fall in Yosemite Valley, but noted that it "excels even that favorite fall both in height and airy-fairy beauty and behavior." Tueeulala Falls is a seasonal waterfall that usually runs dry by late summer, leaving a black, cone-shaped stain on the face of the rock to the left of Wapama Falls.

■ **Wapama Falls** ■ Fed by a much greater volume of water than its ephemeral neighbor, Wapama Falls thunders down the rocks for roughly 1,400 vertical feet. Muir, who often likened the Hetch Hetchy Valley to Yosemite, identified Wapama Falls as the Hetch Hetchy counterpart of Yosemite Falls and described its concussive course through "a jagged, shadowy gorge roaring and thundering, pounding its way like an earthquake avalanche." Standing at the base of the falls at the height of the spring runoff, it is easy to see how Muir might compare Wapama with an earthquake. In some years, the springtime volume of water leads the park service to close the trail beneath the falls.

The unnamed massive cliff between the two waterfalls reminded Muir of another Yosemite Valley landmark: El Capitan.

■ **Kolana Rock** ■ This abrupt snout of granite on the south shore of the reservoir rises nearly 2,000 feet above the water. Muir likened it in position and form to the Cathedral Rocks in Yosemite Valley.

■ **Dusky-footed Wood Rats** ■ A resident of Yosemite's foothills habitat, dusky-footed wood rats build large houses out of sticks, bark, and plant cuttings arranged in conical piles up to eight feet in diameter and eight feet high. Sometimes located beneath bluffs or against or inside trees, these houses are the work of several generations of rats and contain multiple cache chambers where fruit, nuts, seeds, fungi, and various plant materials are stored. The houses are usually occupied by a female and her young. Males live separately, in tree nests. In addition to sheltering the wood rats themselves, the houses often are occupied by other small mammals and various types of frogs, which live in the cache chambers.

Index

Further Reading

Fix, D. and Bezener, A. *Birds of Northern California.* Lone Pine Publishing, Auburn, WA, 2000.

Harris, A., Tuttle, E., and Tuttle, S. *Geology of National Parks,* fifth edition. Kendall/Hunt Publishing, Dubuque, IA, 1997.

Hartesveldt, R., Harvey, H., Shellhammer, H., and Stecker, R. *Giant Sequoias.* Sequoia Natural History Association, Three Rivers, CA, 1981.

Horn, E. *Sierra Nevada Wildflowers.* Mountain Press Publishing Co., Missoula, MT, 1998.

Schaffer, J. *Yosemite National Park: A Natural History Guide to Yosemite and its Trails.* Wilderness Press, Berkeley, CA, 1978.

Soares, M. *100 Hikes in Yosemite National Park.* The Mountaineers Books, Seattle, WA, 2003.

Whitaker, J. *National Audubon Society Field Guide to North American Mammals.* Alfred A. Knopf, NY, 1996.

Wilson L., Wilson J., and Nicholas, J. *Wildflowers of Yosemite.* Sierra Press, Mariposa, CA, 1987.

Thomas Schmidt fell for the Rocky
Mountains as a boy, while spending
summers in the West with his family.
He is the author of six books
about the human and natural history
of the West and has contributed to many other
books published by the National Geographic Society.
He lives in Bozeman, Montana, with his wife,
Terese, and their two children, Pat and Colleen.

Wendy Baylor and Jeremy Schmidt,
  Computer composition and design
Jeremy Schmidt, *Maps*
National Park Service, *Historic photos*

ISBN: 0-7922-5485-6

ISBN-13: 978-0-7922-5485-0

For information about special discounts for bulk purchases, please
contact National Geographic Books Special Sales: ngspecsales@ngs.org